THE
BUSY PEOPLE'S
NATURALLY NUTRITIOUS DECIDEDLY DELICIOUS
FAST FOODBOOK

Sharon Elliot's Recipes

Sandy Haight's Drawings

ACKNOWLEDGEMENTS

Thanks to all of you who so generously offered your enthusiasm and encouragement.
Thanks especially to

Tony Reynolds
Grant Elliot
Lynn Nagel
Abby Neibauer
Suzanne Meek
Barbara Harris
Jerry Martin
Neil Wilkinson
Dean Kolstad
Brent and Megan Elliot
Jacqueline Nagel
Gilbert and Shirley Haight

Copyright © Sharon Elliot and Sandy Haight, 1977

Published by   Fresh Press
                774 Allen Court
                Palo Alto, California 94303

Library of Congress Number: 77-077054
ISBN: 0-9601398-1-8

First Edition: October 1977
Second Printing: January 1978
Third Printing: June 1978

DEDICATION

To all my students and friends who asked,
"What do you have that's fast?"

Natural foods have fun.
They dance
flow
Like to mingle with friends
and create energy...

...natural foods can act impulsively and still come through with good taste. They can form complex combinations or dash off as simple concoctions and still be delicious in passing essential energies to busy people. They enjoy many inspired moments as they form and reform in pursuit of a destiny. They tease our cravings, tantalize our expectations and tempt our impulses to invent new sensations...

CONTENTS

(continued)

SWEET TREATS AND GRATIFYING GOODIES

INTRODUCTION

More and more of today's busy people realize the importance of feeding their bodies well. When buying ''prefab'' food at the supermarket or stopping at a neighborhood fast-food outlet, they regret the nutritional inadequacies, the excessive amounts of fats, sugars and additives, but. . . what else is there? They just don't have the time or the support needed to develop a new food pattern that would free them from this Commercial Fast-Food Syndrome.

THE BUSY PEOPLE'S FOODBOOK offers a reasonable, personally satisfying solution to this dilemma.* Its purpose is to help busy people establish their independence from the excesses and inadequacies of this syndrome without robbing themselves of time wanted for other important concerns and pleasures.

THE BUSY PEOPLE'S FOODBOOK is fast meals from real foods. It's fast because it lends itself to once-a-week, one-stop shopping** and because it makes preparation easy, quick and satisfying. Its foods are real because the main ingredients — fresh fruits and vegetables, yogurt, cheeses, eggs, whole grains, nuts, and milk — are Mother Nature created and Father Time approved. THE FOODBOOK uses a few minimally processed foods — such as frozen concentrated juices, canned tomato products, and powdered milk — because their convenient form encourages their use, thus reducing the nutrient deficiencies most often found in the typical American diet.

Once you've bought THE FOODBOOK's basic ingredients, all manner of good things can be created — either for eating on the spot or for stirring, spreading, dipping, layering, whizzing, or spooning later in the week. You'll become, in essence, your own high-quality, nutrition-conscious, fast-food center. Moreover, taking an active, responsible role in nourishing your body will create new connections between you and your life sources, connections that bring with them a quiet, conscience-heightening joy and a new sense of self-affirmation.

---

* If you are interested in comparing the nutritional adequacy of a Commercial Fast-Food Syndrome day with a BUSY PEOPLE'S FOODBOOK day, see the Four Food Groups' Magic Number System in the appendix.

** To make weekly shopping comprehensive, quick and efficient, a shopping list is extremely helpful. Keep your list and an attached pencil in a convenient place in the kitchen (maybe even taped right to your refrigerator) so you can jot things down when they begin to get low. Doing this will produce a basic list almost automatically. Then, with a few extra minutes spent leafing through THE FOODBOOK, choosing some recipes to make during the week, your list can be rounded out in a short time.

Looking through this foodbook, you'll find healthful variations for lots of familiar foods—shakes that are as tasty as they are nutritious; carbonated drinks that are pluses instead of minuses on your nutrition scorecard; and tangy sundaes that leave you feeling in harmony with yourself rather than logy and maybe even a bit guilt-freckled. Because of THE FOODBOOK's flexible, unconventional ways of dealing with foods, you might also find some new or unusual sounding combinations — tuna and cranberries — peanut butter and cheese — prunes and milk — peaches and ricotta. Save these recipes for days when you have a little extra time for adventuresome fun. Who knows, you might find a new all-time favorite!

Sharon Elliot

ANY MEAL SANDWICHES

Most of us think "lunch" when we hear the word sandwich, but sandwiches can be fun at any meal...hot or cold, open-faced or closed, crunchy or chewy...any way you want them. Just start with a BASE (like bread, toast, corn tortilla*, large cracker, last night's waffle or yesterday's pancake), add a FILLING, and maybe a TOPPER, and there you have it. The fixin's very simple; the variety makes it fun!

*Corn tortillas make great bases for sandwiches. If you like them crispy, but not oily, buy the thinnest ones you can find and "crisp" them in the oven the easy way. Whenever you're using your oven at or below 350°F, make a little room on the rack nearest the middle. Lay some tortillas (flat and separately) right on the rack. Leave them until they are crispy to the touch (5-10 minutes). A few brands want to curl as they crisp — especially if they are frozen when you put them in the oven. Discourage this behavior by gently tucking the edges of the tortillas under the nearby gratings. After the tortillas have crisped and cooled, store them in an airtight container. They'll be ready whenever you are!

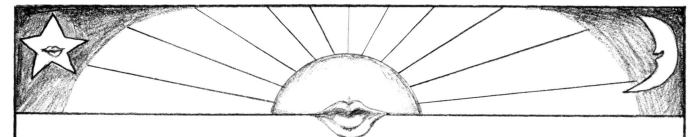

EXPAND YOUR HORIZONS — BREAK THE FAST WITH A SCRUMPTIOUS BREAKFAST SANDWICH!

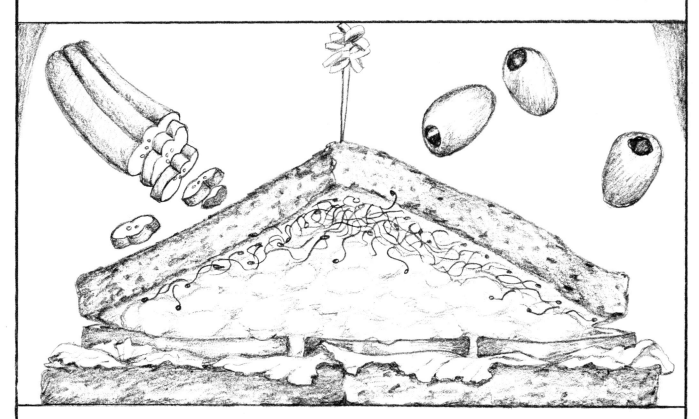

Make a WHOLE-MEALWICH when you find yourself in that "What'll-I-Fix-For-Dinner" Dilemma.

LOCO TORTILLA

Spread about
2 T NATURAL PEANUT BUTTER
gently on a CRISPED TORTILLA.

Eat it right now if you're starving
or turn on your broiler and build
further by adding some
ALFALFA SPROUTS.

Cover the sprouts with
CHEESE (grated or sliced).

Broil about 4" from heat —
just enough to soften the
cheese.

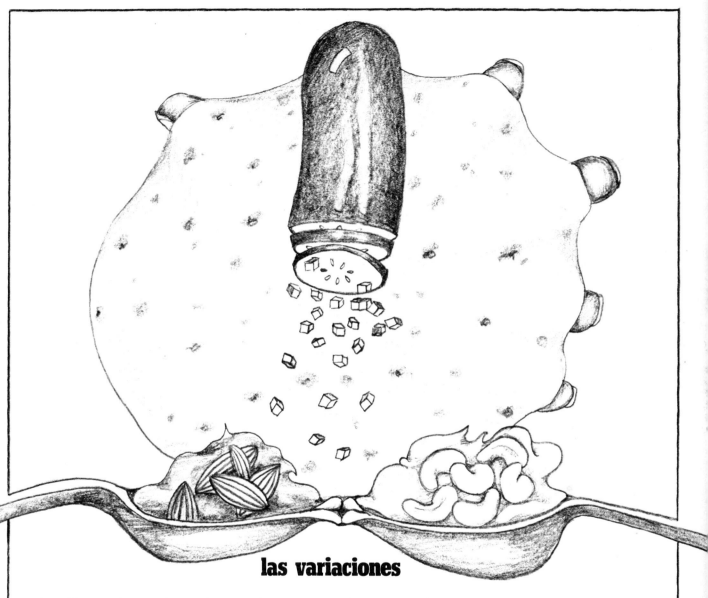

las variaciones

1. Use another nut butter instead of peanut — or blend several kinds together!

2. Replace the sprouts with chopped raw cucumber or any other favorite raw veggie.

3. Try a crispy quesadilla — cover the tortilla generously with cheese and broil until the cheese softens. For a real lip lapper, zap with some chopped green chilis and/or a few avocado slices before adding the cheese.

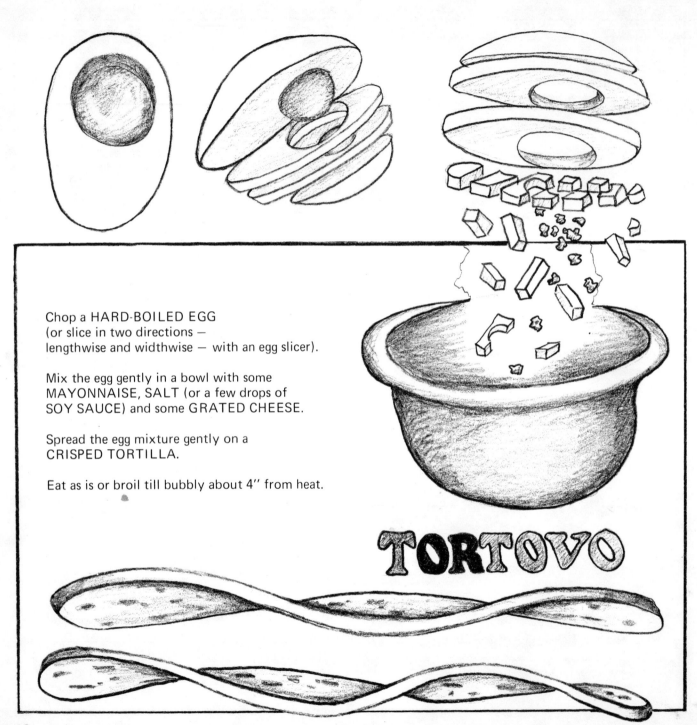

Chop a HARD-BOILED EGG
(or slice in two directions —
lengthwise and widthwise — with an egg slicer).

Mix the egg gently in a bowl with some
MAYONNAISE, SALT (or a few drops of
SOY SAUCE) and some GRATED CHEESE.

Spread the egg mixture gently on a
CRISPED TORTILLA.

Eat as is or broil till bubbly about 4" from heat.

TORTOVO

OR, OR, OR, OR, OR, OR...

1. Add a couple tablespoons of ricotta or cottage cheese to the egg mixture.

2. Sprinkle some chopped walnuts, almonds or peanuts into the egg mixture and fold to blend — or sprinkle them on top of your sandwich just before it's finished broiling and toast the nuts a bit.

3. Wake up your taste buds by mixing a little chili salsa with the mayonnaise. You might even like a few chopped green chilis if you have a flame-retardant tongue!

4. Make a layered TORTOVO by leaving the cheese out of the egg mixture and sprinkling it on top just before broiling.

5. Make a SUPER layered TORTOVO by sandwiching in some sprouts, chopped green onions, green pepper bits, pickle chips, and/or tomato slices between the egg and cheese.

6. Take the "TORT" out of your TORTOVO — use toast or a waffle instead.

MAYONNAISE   CHILE SALSA   COTTAGE CHEESE   SMALL CURD

PIZZA EXPRESS

Spread some TOMATO SAUCE
on a piece of CRISPY TOAST.

Sprinkle with a little
OREGANO and BASIL.

Layer thickly with CHEESE
(grated or sliced).

Broil about 4″ from heat
until bubbly.

viva le variazioni

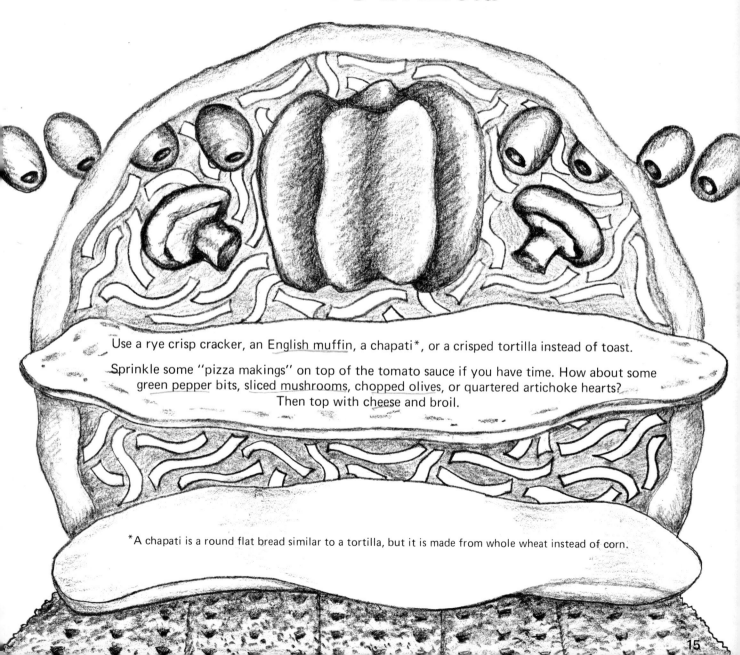

Use a rye crisp cracker, an English muffin, a chapati*, or a crisped tortilla instead of toast.

Sprinkle some "pizza makings" on top of the tomato sauce if you have time. How about some green pepper bits, sliced mushrooms, chopped olives, or quartered artichoke hearts? Then top with cheese and broil.

*A chapati is a round flat bread similar to a tortilla, but it is made from whole wheat instead of corn.

THE GREAT "PEANUT BUTTER AND... FRUITWICH"

Spread about 2 T NATURAL PEANUT BUTTER on your favorite BREAD or TOAST.

Cover with bite-sized APPLE CHUNKS.

Sprinkle with CINNAMON (and NUTMEG too, if you like).

Cover with a thick layer of RICOTTA — top with a swirl or two of HONEY for a super-sweet sensation!

Also Starring:

1. The Broiled Fruitwich — really hot in the part!
2. Jack, Cheddar, or Muenster — understudies to Ricotta.
3. Banana Rounds or Dried Fruit Bits — stand-ins for Apple Chunks.
4. Sunflower Seeds, Pumpkin Seeds, and/or Soy Nuts crowning Peanut Butter in evening performances.
5. The World Renowned DOUBLE-DEALING, SWEET-APPEALING GREAT PEANUT BUTTER PUT-ON — ssh-ssh-ssh — it's Almond Butter or Tahini playing Peanut Butter's part.

FORKERS

Spread several tablespoons of last night's REFRIED or BAKED BEANS* on your favorite dark BREAD, TOAST, or CORNBREAD.

Cover with a thick layer of RICOTTA, GRATED CHEESE, or both.

Enjoy as is or broil about 4" from heat to soften the cheese.

*Either use the traditional saucepan means to rewarm the beans or put them in the broiler about 8–10" from the heat after you have spread them on your bread. They'll warm while you get the cheeses ready!

BEANY BREAD

Cottage Toast

Mix 1/4 c COTTAGE CHEESE
with 2 T GRATED CHEESE.

Add some SEEDS — sesame,
poppy, or caraway — if you like.

Spread the cheese on TOAST
or on a THICK TOMATO SLICE.

Eat as is or broil till bubbly
about 4″ from heat.

QUICK FISHWICH

Mix 2-3 ounces of ALBACORE TUNA or BONITA with a little MAYONNAISE and ONION POWDER.

Spread it all on a piece of TOAST.

Broil about 4'' from heat till tuna tips start to brown a bit.

¿WHICH FISH?

1. Cover the tuna with sprouts and cheese. Then broil.
2. Use salmon instead of tuna.
3. Add a chopped hard-boiled egg, some grated cheese, and/or some dill pickle chips to the fish mixture — even celery is good in a crunch.

SALMON

FAROUT FORKERS

TOMWICH

Spread TOAST or BREAD with MAYONNAISE and prepared or Dijon MUSTARD.

Layer with TOMATO SLICES.

Top with PICKLE CHIPS.

Sprinkle generously with GRATED CHEESE.

Broil till bubbly about 4" from heat.

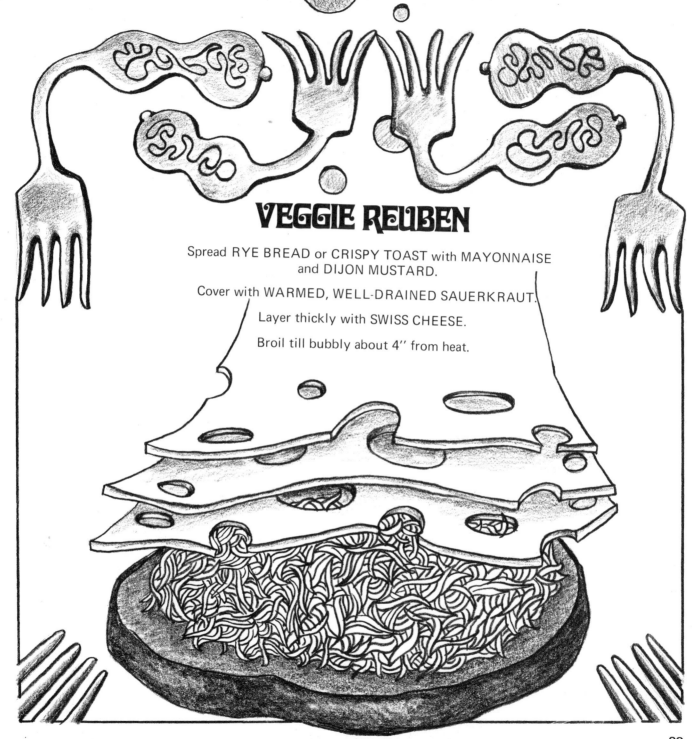

VEGGIE REUBEN

Spread RYE BREAD or CRISPY TOAST with MAYONNAISE and DIJON MUSTARD.

Cover with WARMED, WELL-DRAINED SAUERKRAUT.

Layer thickly with SWISS CHEESE.

Broil till bubbly about 4'' from heat.

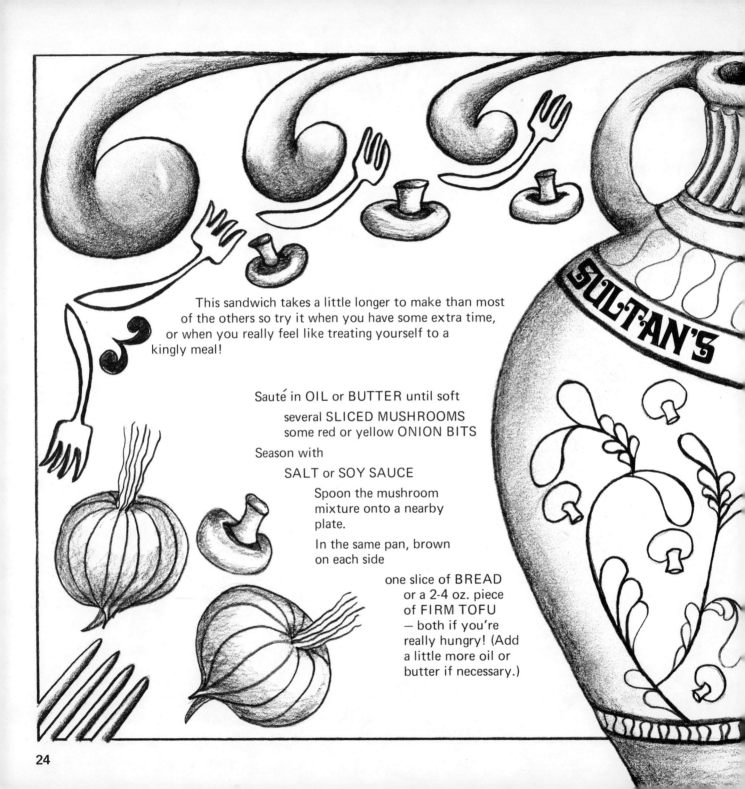

This sandwich takes a little longer to make than most of the others so try it when you have some extra time, or when you really feel like treating yourself to a kingly meal!

Sauté in OIL or BUTTER until soft

several SLICED MUSHROOMS
some red or yellow ONION BITS

Season with

SALT or SOY SAUCE

Spoon the mushroom mixture onto a nearby plate.

In the same pan, brown on each side

one slice of BREAD or a 2-4 oz. piece of FIRM TOFU — both if you're really hungry! (Add a little more oil or butter if necessary.)

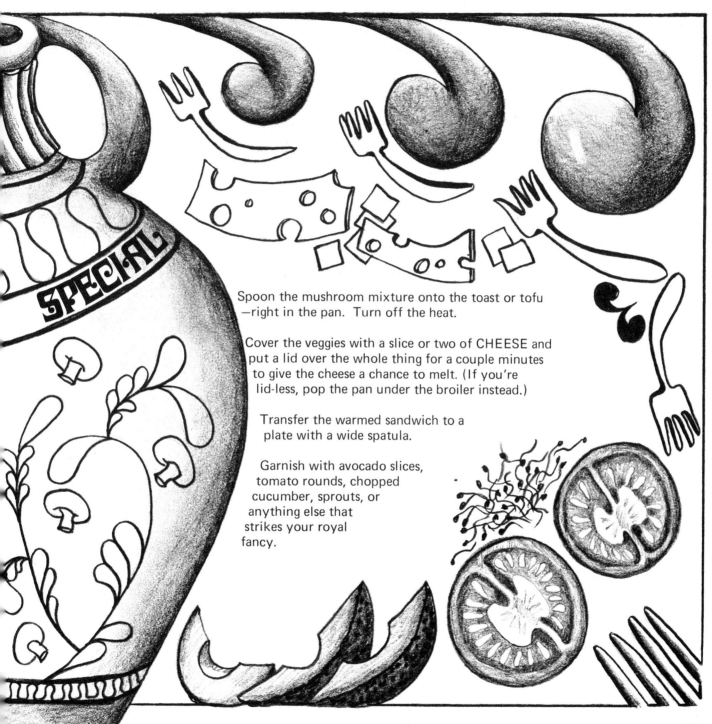

Spoon the mushroom mixture onto the toast or tofu
—right in the pan. Turn off the heat.

Cover the veggies with a slice or two of CHEESE and
put a lid over the whole thing for a couple minutes
to give the cheese a chance to melt. (If you're
lid-less, pop the pan under the broiler instead.)

Transfer the warmed sandwich to a
plate with a wide spatula.

Garnish with avocado slices,
tomato rounds, chopped
cucumber, sprouts, or
anything else that
strikes your royal
fancy.

SPECIAL

BLENDER QUENCHERS

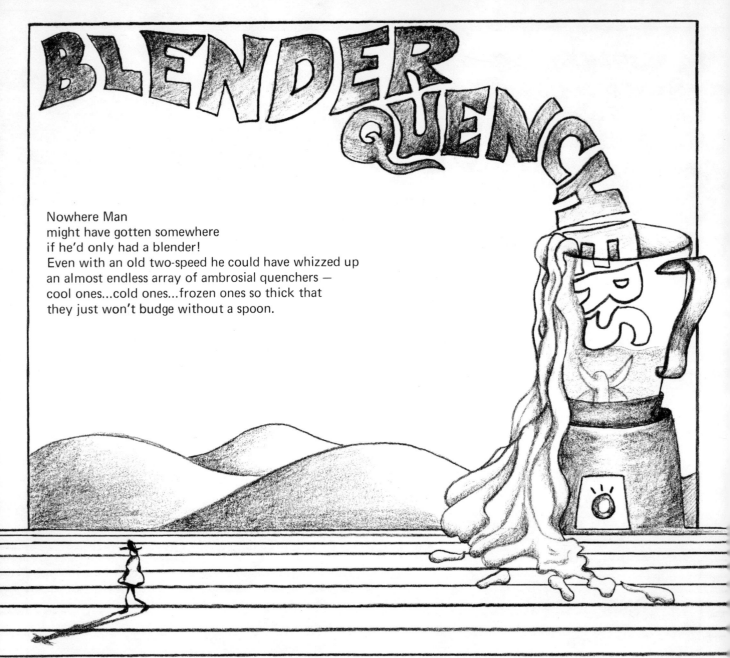

BLENDER QUENCHERS

Nowhere Man
might have gotten somewhere
if he'd only had a blender!
Even with an old two-speed he could have whizzed up
an almost endless array of ambrosial quenchers —
cool ones...cold ones...frozen ones so thick that
they just won't budge without a spoon.

If, upon first tasting these ambrosial quenchers, you find that you have an undeveloped taste bud or two,
add a little extra sweetening. As time goes on, though, think your taste buds to maturity — LICK THAT HABIT!

GOOD MORNING!

Measure 1 c PLAIN YOGURT into your blender.

Add 2–3 T FROZEN ORANGE JUICE CONCENTRATE.

Blend just enough to mix. (If your yogurt is really thick you might want to thin it a bit with milk.)

For a real eye-opener, try adding 1/3–1/2 of a very ripe banana and/or 1/2 T nutritional (not baking) yeast before you blend. Don't start out with 1/2 T if you haven't had much yeast before, though. Work up to it slowly — preferably over a few weeks time — by starting with about 1/4 t the first few times. Yeast is a great, nutrient-rich food, but if you aren't used to it, your system could complain loudly!!

Pineapple Feathers

Measure 3/4 c PLAIN YOGURT into the blender.

Add

    3 T (4 if you're a real pineapple lover)
    FROZEN PINEAPPLE JUICE CONCENTRATE.

Blend just enough to mix.

EARLY BIRD INSPIRATIONS

1.   Add 1/3 of a very ripe banana and/or a sprinkle of nutmeg.

2.   Substitute buttermilk for the yogurt — different and delicious!

Pink Tomato

Measure 1/4 c PLAIN YOGURT into your blender.

Pour in 1 c TOMATO JUICE.

Add
    a shake of GARLIC POWDER
    a few drops of WORCHESTERSHIRE SAUCE
    about 1/16th of SALT

Blend to mix.

Added bits of cucumber and/or green pepper
make PINK TOMATO a great, chilled "Spoonin' Soup".

Orange Chiller

Measure 1 c LOWFAT MILK into your blender.

Add
    2 T (heaping)   INSTANT NONFAT POWDERED MILK
    2 T (heaping)   FROZEN ORANGE JUICE CONCENTRATE

Blend just enough to mix.

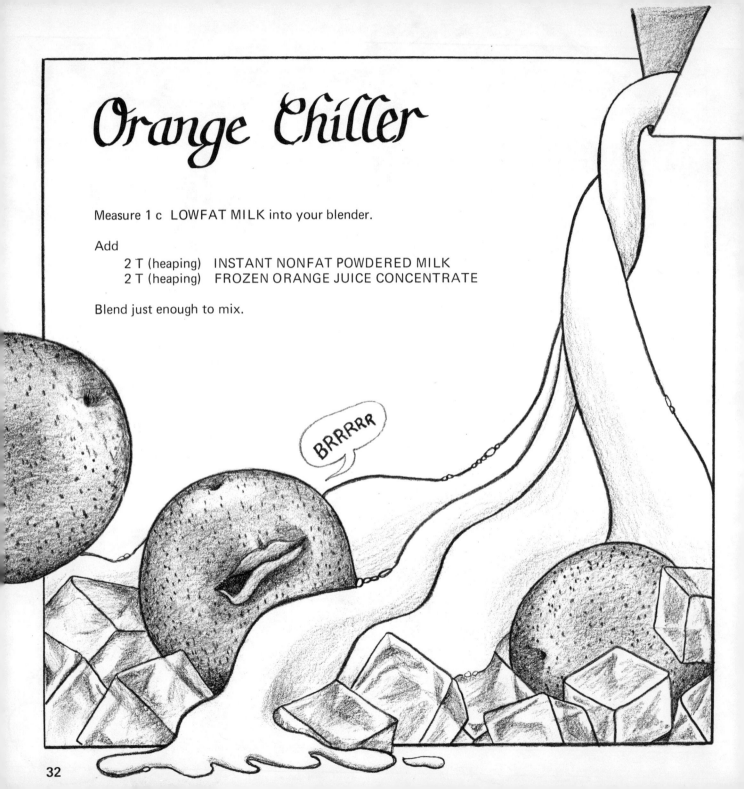

Prunella

Measure 3/4 c LOWFAT MILK into the blender.

Add
      1/4 c   PITTED PRUNES (about five)
      1 t   UNSULPHURED MOLASSES
            (the "un-bitter one")

Blend until the prunes are an integral part of your drink.

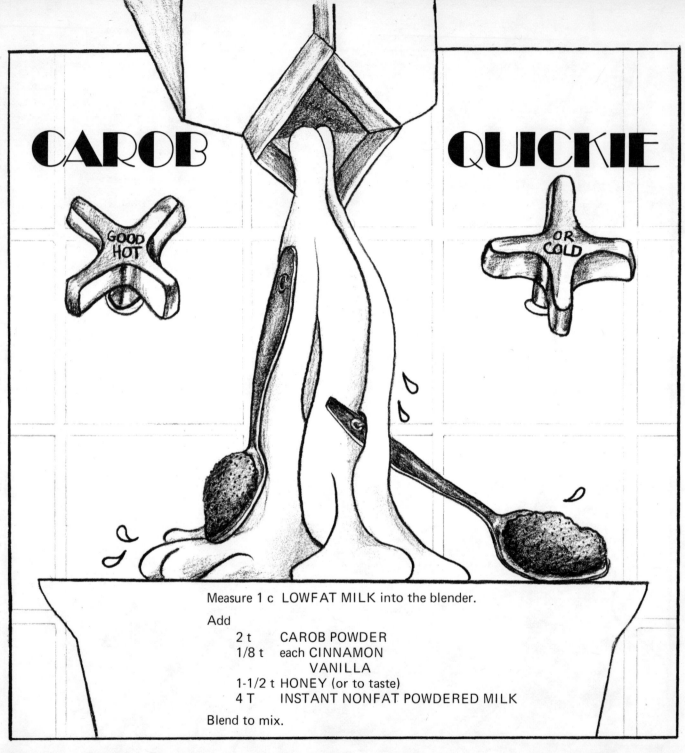

CAROB QUICKIE

GOOD HOT

OR COLD

Measure 1 c LOWFAT MILK into the blender.

Add

2 t	CAROB POWDER	
1/8 t	each CINNAMON	
	VANILLA	
1-1/2 t	HONEY (or to taste)	
4 T	INSTANT NONFAT POWDERED MILK	

Blend to mix.

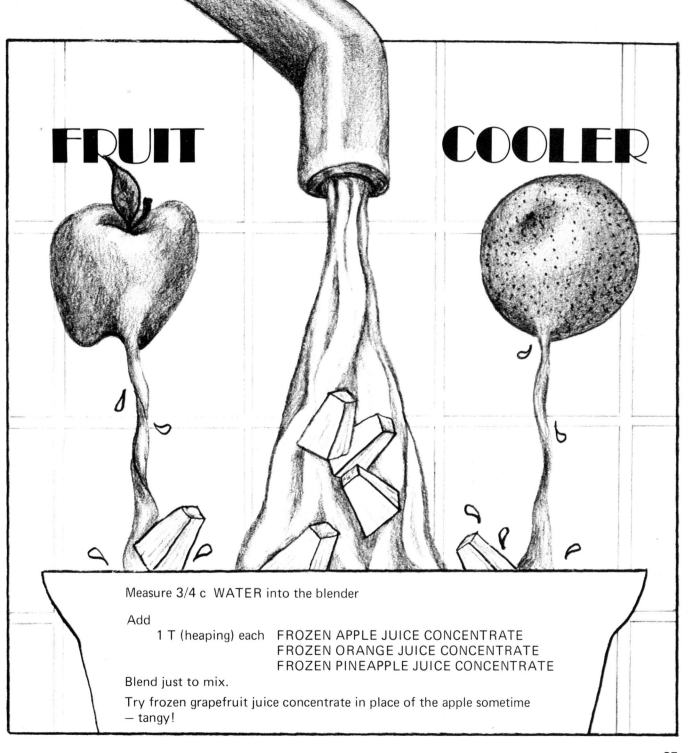

FRUIT COOLER

Measure 3/4 c WATER into the blender

Add

1 T (heaping) each   FROZEN APPLE JUICE CONCENTRATE
FROZEN ORANGE JUICE CONCENTRATE
FROZEN PINEAPPLE JUICE CONCENTRATE

Blend just to mix.

Try frozen grapefruit juice concentrate in place of the apple sometime
— tangy!

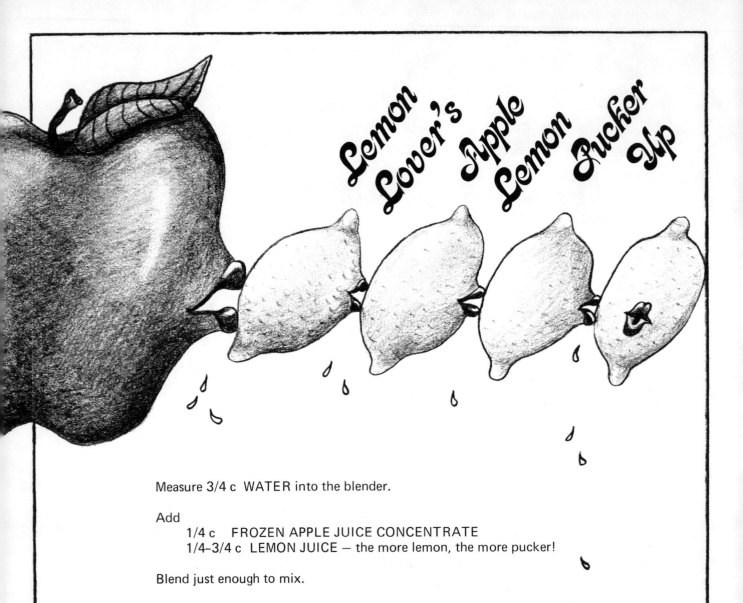

Lemon Lover's Apple Lemon Pucker Up

Measure 3/4 c WATER into the blender.

Add
    1/4 c   FROZEN APPLE JUICE CONCENTRATE
    1/4–3/4 c LEMON JUICE — the more lemon, the more pucker!

Blend just enough to mix.

FRUIT BUBBLE
(the un-blender drink)

Try reconstituting any frozen juice with a natural, carbonated mineral water such as Calistoga, or part tap water and part carbonated water. Re---freshing!

BRENT'S BUBBLE

Measure into a tall glass and mix well
    1/4 c FROZEN GRAPEFRUIT CONCENTRATE
    1/2 c TAP WATER

Add
    1/4 c CALISTOGA WATER

Stir gently.

Vary the amounts of tap and Calistoga water to suit your own Bubble P.Q.*

*Pleasure Quotient

Now that you've got the hang of it, go creative! Indulge your own Blender Quencher imagination.

Just combine a base with a flavoring and/or a sparker and a sweetener — taste — adjust — enjoy.

BASES

yogurt   milk
        powdered milk and water
buttermilk   fruit juice
    About 1/2-3/4 c per serving

SPARKERS AND SWEETNERS

maple syrup   cinnamon   very ripe bananas

nutmeg   vanilla   honey

date bits   lemon juice   lemon peel

raisins

FLAVORINGS

fresh or frozen fruit —
peaches, bananas, berries, etc.

About 1/2 c per serving

or

frozen fruit juice concentrate —
orange, apple, apple cider, pineapple,
pineapple-orange, grapefruit, etc.

About 2 T per serving

Is your blender intimidated by the very mention of the words "ice cubes"?
Does it seem to cry out, "I can't, I can't", before it has even tried?

Increase your blender's self-confidence today! Use Dr. Braveblender's
foolproof ANY-BLENDER-CAN-HANDLE-THOSE-ICE-CUBES TECHNIQUE.

Dr. Braveblender says

ALWAYS mix and taste-test your drink before you add any ice —
be especially careful not to slight Honey by trying to introduce
her to an icy cold drink or she'll just **never** loosen up!

ALWAYS have your drink whizzing around at top speed in the
blender when you begin to add the ice.

ALWAYS put the large part of your blender's cap on tight — and
how about some cotton in your ears, too, if they're sensitive?

ALWAYS feed your blender its ice cubes ONE AT A TIME by
dropping them through the little opening in the cap — keep your
hand over the opening if you're not up for an occasional wet kiss!

IF you run across a stubborn ice cube that just refuses to accept
its new identity, try turning your blender off and on quickly a
few times to give the stubborn cube a good tossing.

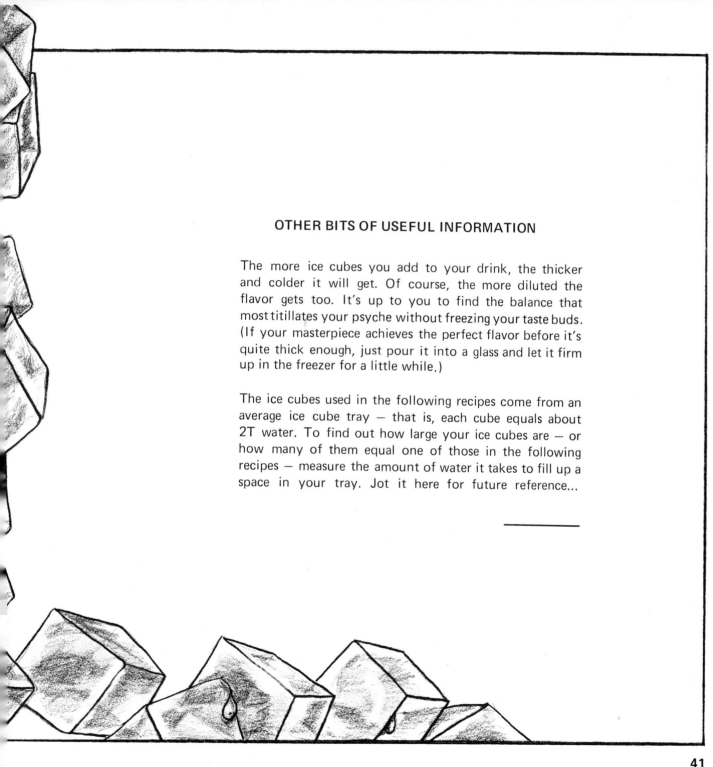

OTHER BITS OF USEFUL INFORMATION

The more ice cubes you add to your drink, the thicker and colder it will get. Of course, the more diluted the flavor gets too. It's up to you to find the balance that most titillates your psyche without freezing your taste buds. (If your masterpiece achieves the perfect flavor before it's quite thick enough, just pour it into a glass and let it firm up in the freezer for a little while.)

The ice cubes used in the following recipes come from an average ice cube tray — that is, each cube equals about 2T water. To find out how large your ice cubes are — or how many of them equal one of those in the following recipes — measure the amount of water it takes to fill up a space in your tray. Jot it here for future reference...

BANANA FROSTY

Measure 1 c LOWFAT MILK into your blender.

Add

2/3 c	INSTANT NONFAT POWDERED MILK
1/2 t	VANILLA
1	VERY RIPE BANANA*

Blend until the banana is thoroughly mixed. Taste for sweetness. Add a little honey if necessary, then blend again.

With your blender running on high, drop 4 ICE CUBES, one at a time, through the little cap in the top of your blender.

Blend just until the ice is an integral part of your drink.

Serve at once.

*Very ripe bananas make fantastic sweeteners for blender drinks. You can always recognize a VRB by its well-freckled skin and its soft, aromatic insides.

PEANUT BUTTER-PERO SHAKE

Measure 3/4 c LOWFAT MILK into the blender.

Add

1/2 c	INSTANT NONFAT POWDERED MILK
3 T	PEANUT BUTTER
1 T	HONEY (or to taste)
1 t	PERO*

Blend well. Scrape down the sides of your blender if necessary.

Taste for sweetness and adjust.

With the blender running on high, drop 2 ICE CUBES, one at a time, through the little cap in the top of your blender.

Blend just until the ice is an integral part of your drink.

Serve at once.

*Pero is an instant coffee substitute made from barley, chickory, rye and a bit of molasses — tasty and no caffeine!

43

CAROB SHAKE

Measure 1 c LOWFAT MILK into your blender.

Add

2/3 c	INSTANT NONFAT POWDERED MILK
1 T	CAROB POWDER
1/8 t	CINNAMON
1/4 t	VANILLA
1-1/2 t	HONEY (or to taste)

Blend well.

With your blender running on high, drop 4 ICE CUBES, one at a time, through the little cap in the top of your blender.

Blend just until the ice is an integral part of your drink.

Serve at once.

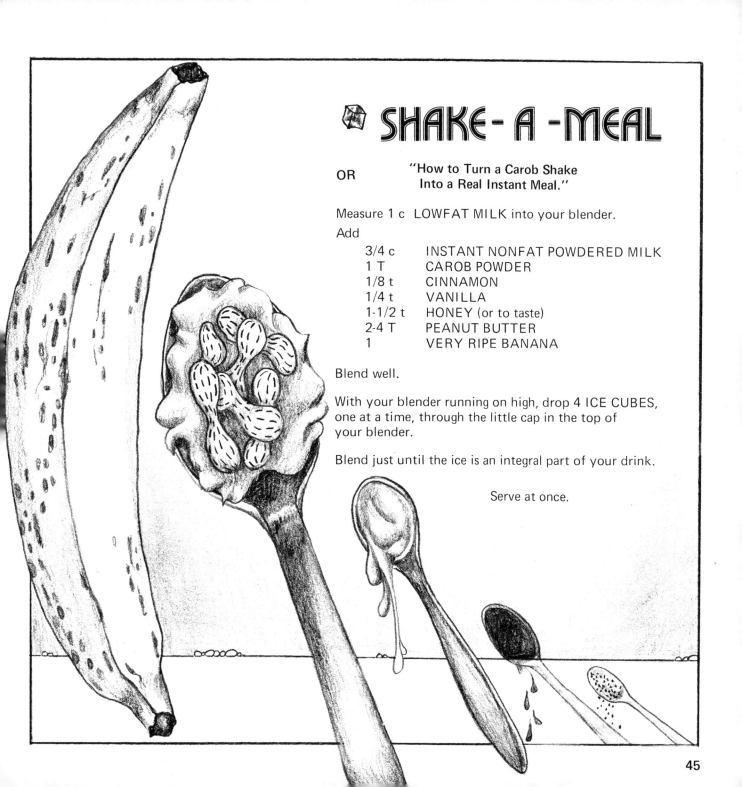

SHAKE-A-MEAL

OR "How to Turn a Carob Shake
Into a Real Instant Meal."

Measure 1 c LOWFAT MILK into your blender.
Add

3/4 c	INSTANT NONFAT POWDERED MILK
1 T	CAROB POWDER
1/8 t	CINNAMON
1/4 t	VANILLA
1-1/2 t	HONEY (or to taste)
2-4 T	PEANUT BUTTER
1	VERY RIPE BANANA

Blend well.

With your blender running on high, drop 4 ICE CUBES,
one at a time, through the little cap in the top of
your blender.

Blend just until the ice is an integral part of your drink.

Serve at once.

Strawberry Slurper

Measure 3/4 c LOWFAT MILK into your blender.

Add
    1/2 c   INSTANT NONFAT POWDERED MILK
    1 T   HONEY or 1/2 of a VERY RIPE BANANA
           (or both)
    a few drops of VANILLA

Blend until well mixed.

With the blender running on high, drop 10-12
FROZEN UNSWEETENED STRAWBERRIES (about 1
heaping cupful), one at a time, through the little cap in
the top of your blender.

Blend just until the berries are an integral part of
your drink.

Serve at once.

Apple Snow Spooner

If your teeth can take it, you can make any reconstituted drink super-spoonin' cold just by substituting ice cubes for some of the water needed to reconstitute.

Instead of having a glass of ordinary apple juice, test your mettle with an APPLE SNOW SPOONER.

Measure 1/2 c WATER into your blender.

Add 6 T FROZEN APPLE JUICE CONCENTRATE
(1/2 a small 6 oz. can)

Blend to mix.

With the blender running on high, drop 8-10 ICE CUBES, one at a time, through the little cap in the top of your blender.

Blend just until your drink is the consistency of snow.

Try any of your favorite frozen fruit drinks as spooners — especially great under the Old Oak Tree on a hot summer day!

in a hurry?

DASHING BOWLERS

Yogurt Sundae

Help yourself to a large bowl. Fill it about 1/2 full with PLAIN YOGURT.

Spoon on some partially defrosted FROZEN JUICE CONCENTRATE (orange, apple, etc.)

or

STEWED DRIED FRUIT

or

FRESH FRUIT of your choice (except for pineapple or kiwi, which will react with the yogurt in about fifteen minutes and completely dash your Bowler!)

Stir. (optional)

Sprinkle with NUTS, SEEDS, OATS, and/or GRANOLA.

Apricot Super Sundae

Measure 1 c PLAIN YOGURT into a bowl.

Stir in 2 T FROZEN PINEAPPLE JUICE CONCENTRATE
or   1-2 T FROZEN APPLE JUICE CONCENTRATE (optional)

Add 1/2 c cold STEWED APRICOTS or some APRICOT BUTTER
(see recipe page 92) and marble into the yogurt.

Add some "SPRINKLES" (See YOGURT SUNDAE.)

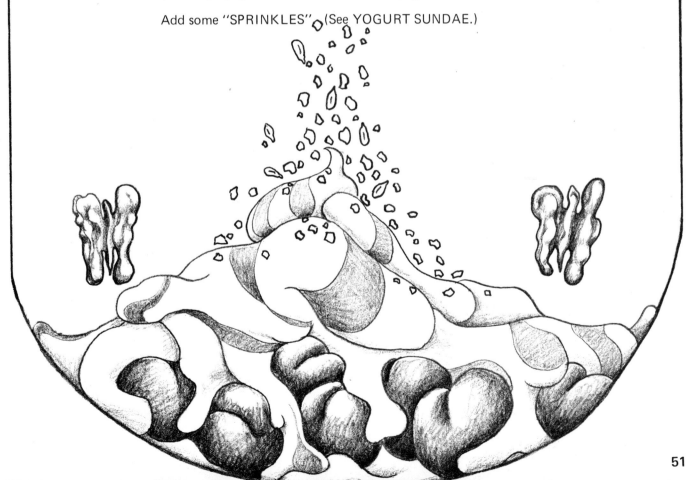

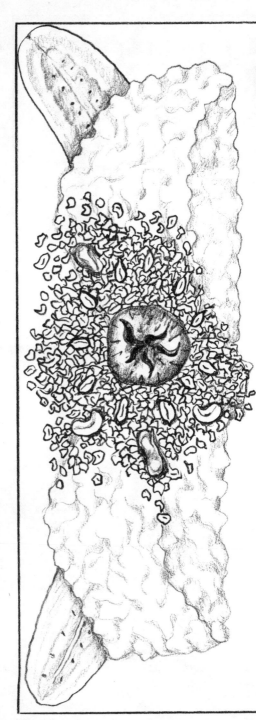

Granola Split

Spoon two mounds of
COTTAGE CHEESE into a
bowl — use an ice cream scoop
if you want to be fancy!

Cut half a BANANA into
fingers and lay them alongside
the cheese.

Sprinkle everything generously
with "the works".

OATS

GRANOLA

NUTS

and/or

SEEDS

Top your split with some
FRESH CRUSHED FRUIT
or a few generous scoops of
FROZEN JUICE
CONCENTRATE.

(For that authentic, gooey-
sundae look, give the
concentrate a few minutes
to soften and drizzle down
your split's sides.)

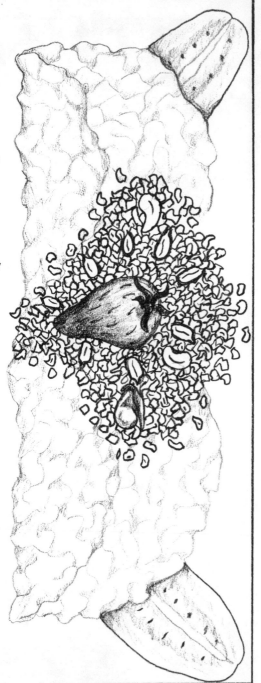

Peachy Ricotta

Spoon 1/2 c RICOTTA
into a bowl.

Pour on 1 c FRESH PEACH
SLICES, slightly mashed so
they're extra juicy.

Mix gently.

Sprinkle with "the works".
OATS
GRANOLA
NUTS
and/or
SEEDS

MOO SALAD

Mix 1/2 c COTTAGE CHEESE or RICOTTA (or some of both) with a CHOPPED HARD-BOILED EGG.

Stir in some TOMATO BITS, CUCUMBER CHIPS, GREEN PEPPER SQUARES, and/or CHOPPED NUTS and SALT.

Top with a mound of ALFALFA SPROUTS or a sprinkle of GRATED CHEESE.

ENCORES GALORE!

Mix or layer cottage cheese, yogurt, and/or ricotta with last night's bean or veggie main dish.

Top with alfalfa sprouts, grated cheese, raw vegetable slices, chopped nuts, or anything else that tantalizes your taste buds.

Give leftovers a better place in life — call them "Encores" and you'll never deal with a lonely, lowly left-over again.

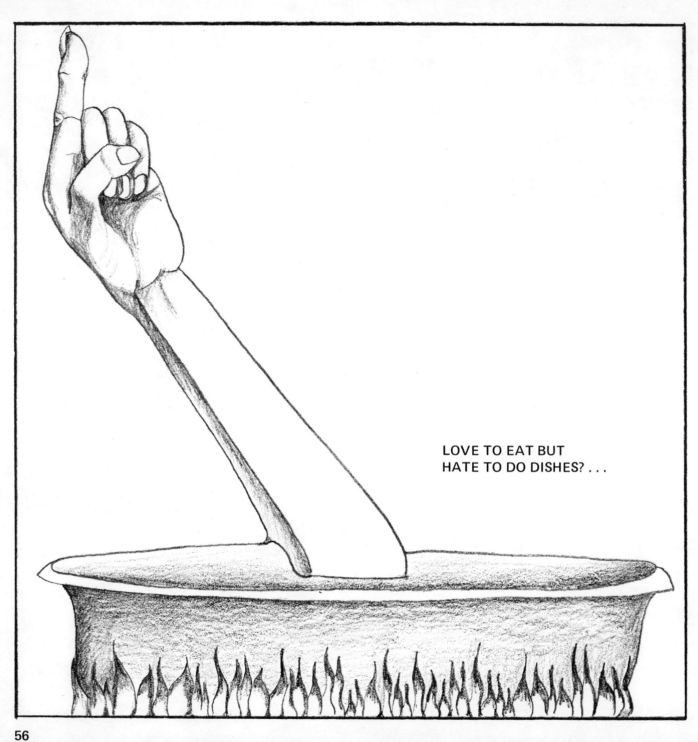

LOVE TO EAT BUT
HATE TO DO DISHES? . . .

ONE PAN PLANS

1

Mix well in a blender or a small bowl
3 EGGS   dash SALT
1-1/2 T MILK   1/8 t DILL WEED

Scramble the eggs over low heat. When they begin to set, crumble on 3-4 oz. WELL-DRAINED ALBACORE TUNA (1/2 a small can).

Cover the tuna with GRATED CHEESE.

Remove the pan from heat and cover until the cheese melts.

Serve in pie wedges.

Serves two.

Mushroom Shrimp Sauté

Sauté in OIL or BUTTER until soft
1/2 lb. SLICED MUSHROOMS
Add
1 c   COOKED SHRIMP (canned is O.K.)
3 T   SHERRY
Heat through.
Good as is or served over warm rice.
Enough for two.

Mushruna Ricotta

Sauté in OIL until soft
1 LARGE ONION, chopped
1/2 lb. THICKLY SLICED MUSHROOMS

Add

1 c   RICOTTA (1/2 lb.)
6 oz.   UNDRAINED, WATER-PACKED
         ALBACORE TUNA (optional)
1/2 t   SALT (or to taste)

Heat just enough to warm through.

Good served with — or even stirred into —
baby green peas.

Plenty for two.

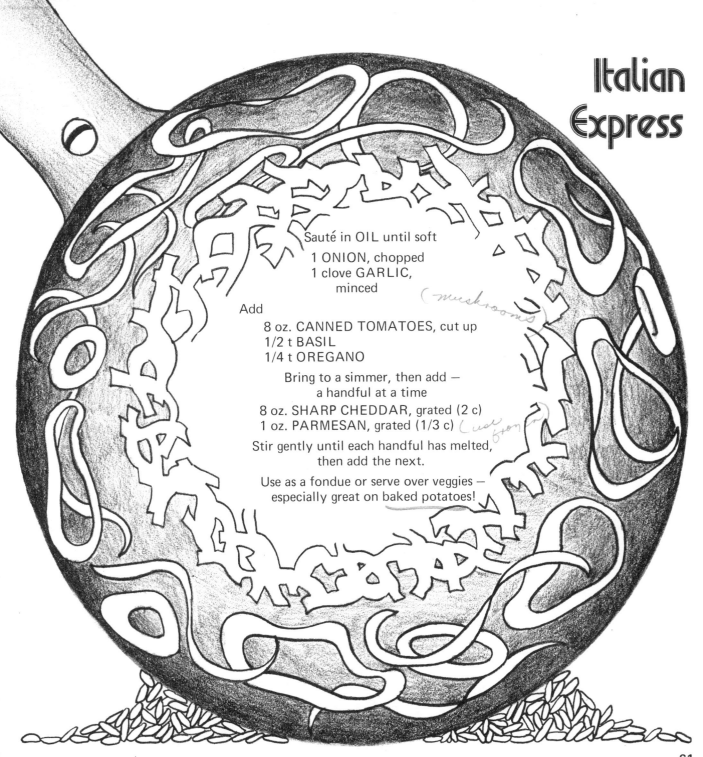

Italian Express

Sauté in OIL until soft

1 ONION, chopped
1 clove GARLIC,
   minced

(mushrooms)

Add

   8 oz. CANNED TOMATOES, cut up
   1/2 t BASIL
   1/4 t OREGANO

   Bring to a simmer, then add —
     a handful at a time

8 oz. SHARP CHEDDAR, grated (2 c)
1 oz. PARMESAN, grated (1/3 c) *(use from)*

Stir gently until each handful has melted,
   then add the next.

Use as a fondue or serve over veggies —
   especially great on baked potatoes!

REFRIGERATOR READIES

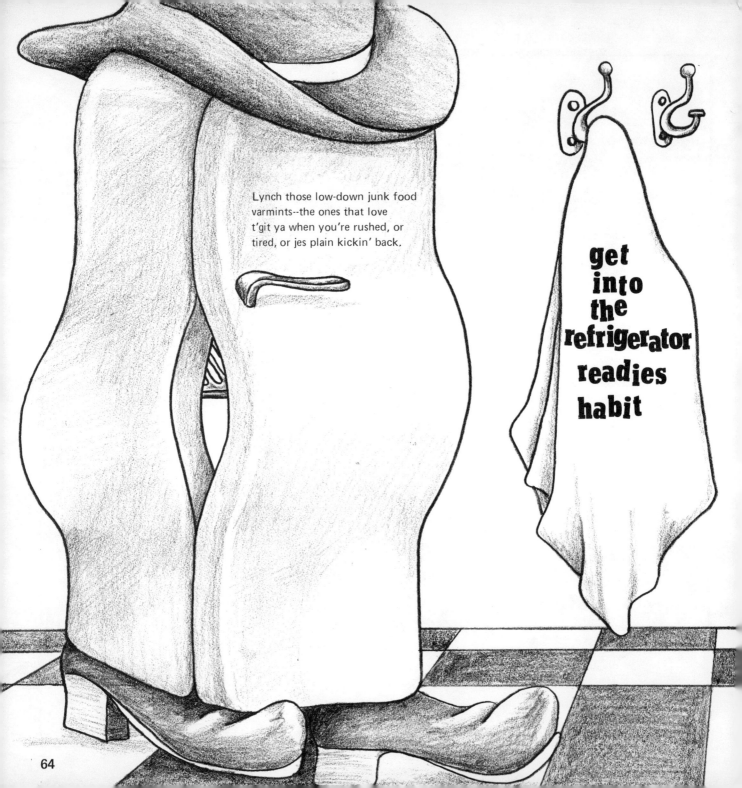

Lynch those low-down junk food
varmints--the ones that love
t'git ya when you're rushed, or
tired, or jes plain kickin' back.

**get
into
the
refrigerator
readies
habit**

REFRIGERATOR READIES

Say "so long" to cold, bare shelves — with RR's your fridge will be a showplace!

Give me a minute to pull myself together

RR's do need a little help getting themselves together, but they're very flexible and will cooperate almost any time you're in the mood. (Compulsive folks love to prepare RR's at the first sign of a midweek slump or an otherwise do-nothing weekend morning.)

Even cleaning up after RR's can be super easy if you do your mixing right in a container that has a tight fitting lid — mix, cover, and refrigerate — just a spoon or two to wash!

65

Clam Ricotta

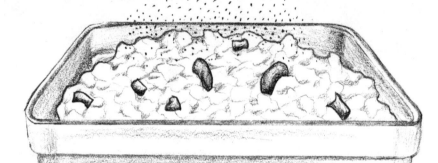

Mix in a container

      6-7 oz. UNDRAINED MINCED CLAMS
           (one small can)
      1/2 t   SALT (or to taste)
      1/8 t each   GARLIC POWDER
                 CELERY SEED
                 ONION POWDER

Add

      1 lb.   RICOTTA

Blend thoroughly. Snap on the cover and refrigerate until needed.

Will be tasty for 3-7 days in the fridge.

Good spooned from a bowl, used as a salad dressing, served as a veggie dip, or spread on well-crisped toast squares and broiled.

If you're having a party, fill bite-sized cream puffs with CLAM RICOTTA — great hors d'oeuvres.

Persian Soup

Mix in a quart container

2 c	PLAIN YOGURT
1/4-1/2 t	SALT
1 c	CHOPPED CUCUMBER
	(1/2 a medium-large one)
1/4 c	CHOPPED WALNUTS

Stir gently. Cover and refrigerate until needed.

Keeps up to a week.

Serve in a mug or stemmed goblet. Garnish with chopped green onion or an extra bit of chopped walnut.

(Remember the Granola Split)

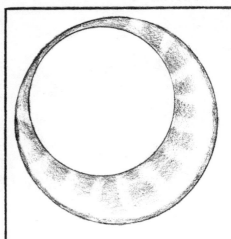

If you don't have time to split a banana, how about just mixing some NUTS and DATES (or RAISINS) with the COTTAGE CHEESE you find left in your refrigerator. Then when you need an emergency pick-up, voila! All you need is a spoon.

You can even make a quick dessert out of some of your emergency provisions by adding a little FROZEN APPLE JUICE CONCENTRATE and a couple sprinkles of CINNAMON (NUTMEG too?) before you dig in.

Sweet Delight

Make a super dessert or sweet spread by mixing CREAM CHEESE (or RICOTTA) with lots of DATE BITS and coarsely CHOPPED NUTS — walnuts or almonds are especially good.

Best after flavors have blended for at least a few hours in the fridge.

Keeps 3-7 days when ricotta is used; keeps a long time when you use cream cheese.

honey orange cream

Mix in a container

        3 T (scant)   DEFROSTED FROZEN ORANGE JUICE CONCENTRATE
        2 t   HONEY
        some   CHOPPED WALNUT BITS

Add

        1 c   CREAM CHEESE

Stir thoroughly. Store in fridge. Keeps well.

Spread on bread or crackers — great on gingerbread!

apple almond cream

Mix in a container

1 T (heaping)	DEFROSTED FROZEN APPLE JUICE CONCENTRATE
2 t	HONEY
2 dashes	CINNAMON
16	ALMONDS, chopped fine

Add

1 c	CREAM CHEESE

Stir thoroughly. Store in fridge. Keeps well.

Great with fruit, on a crisp cracker, or for a sweet sandwich.

SWEET CHEESE

Combine in a medium-sized container

    1/2 c   GRATED WHITE CHEDDAR (2 oz.)
    1/3-1/2 c CHOPPED DATES

Mix or knead until well blended. Add salt if desired and a little mayonnaise or honey to help hold it all together if it seems to need it.

Store in the fridge. Keeps a long time.

Great in sandwiches, on crackers, or even "spooned".

Try substituting raisins or currants for the dates sometimes.

NUTTY CHEESE

Want to try your cheese nutty instead of sweet?

Substitute chopped nuts for the date pieces in SWEET CHEESE — experiment until you find your favorite nut/cheese (or even seed/cheese) combination.

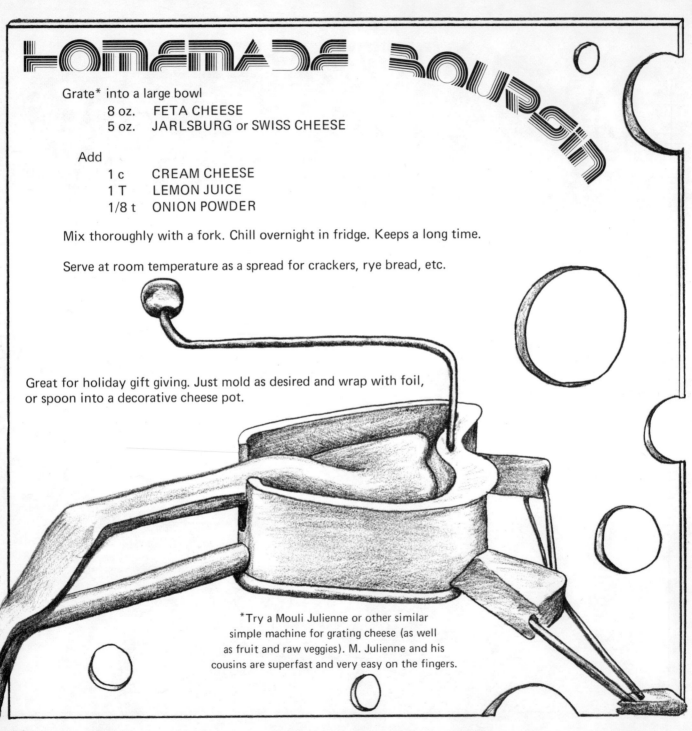

HOMEMADE BOURSIN

Grate* into a large bowl
- 8 oz.   FETA CHEESE
- 5 oz.   JARLSBURG or SWISS CHEESE

Add
- 1 c   CREAM CHEESE
- 1 T   LEMON JUICE
- 1/8 t   ONION POWDER

Mix thoroughly with a fork. Chill overnight in fridge. Keeps a long time.

Serve at room temperature as a spread for crackers, rye bread, etc.

Great for holiday gift giving. Just mold as desired and wrap with foil, or spoon into a decorative cheese pot.

*Try a Mouli Julienne or other similar simple machine for grating cheese (as well as fruit and raw veggies). M. Julienne and his cousins are superfast and very easy on the fingers.

APPLE CHEESE

Mix in a medium-sized bowl

2 c	GRATED WHITE CHEDDAR (1/2 lb.)
2 T	WHOLE WHEAT FLOUR

In a small saucepan combine

3/4 c	WATER
1/2 c	FROZEN APPLE JUICE CONCENTRATE
dash	SALT
1/16 t each	NUTMEG
	MACE
	CINNAMON

Bring the apple juice mixture almost to a boil. Turn the heat to low and add the cheese, 1/4 c at a time, stirring to melt completely before adding more.

Cook and stir over low heat until thick and glossy — about 3 minutes.

Store in a covered container in the fridge. Keeps a week or more.

Great served as a warm fondue with pippin apple slices (dipped in lemon juice to prevent browning), fresh mushrooms, raw zucchini rounds, and jicama fingers.

Mix in a container

1/3 c	TAHINI or SESAME BUTTER
2 T	HONEY
1/2 t	CINNAMON
1-2 T	WATER (if needed to reach desired consistency)

Store covered in the refrigerator. Keeps a long time.

Serve either cold or at room temperature as a dip or topping for fresh fruit, like bananas and apples, or make it thick and use it as a spread in a DOUBLE-DEALING, SWEET-APPEALING GREAT PEANUT BUTTER PUT-ON! (See page 17.)

TAHINI FRUIT TOPPER

Mix in a container (or blend smooth in your blender)

2/3 c   YOGURT
1/3 c   TAHINI or SESAME BUTTER
2 T   LEMON JUICE
a dash or two of GARLIC POWDER

Blend well. Store covered in the fridge. Keeps for ten days or more.

Serve either cold or at room temperature — whichever you like better.
Spoon "SPOON-IT" over salads, cottage cheese, or cooked veggies.
Better yet, just spoon it — your mouth will love you for it!

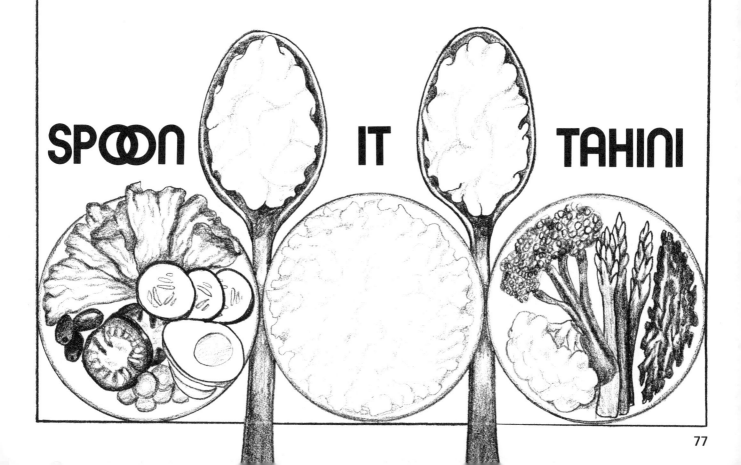

SPOON IT TAHINI

PESOYTA

Mix in a container

      1/4 c   TAHINI or SESAME BUTTER
      2 T   PEANUT BUTTER

  Add

      1/4 c   SOY NUTS, chopped fine or
                crushed with a rolling pin.

Blend well.

Store covered in the fridge. Keeps a long time.

Use PESOYTA on crackers, in lettuce leaf roll-ups, or in
sandwiches with alfalfa sprouts and/or other crispy raw vegetables.

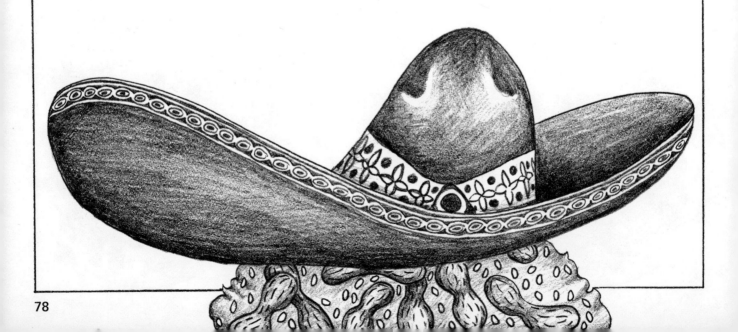

Measure into your blender

     1 c   COTTAGE CHEESE
     1 c   RICOTTA
     1/2 t SEASONED SALT

Chameleon Cheese

Add

     4 oz.   PARMESAN, cut into small pieces

Blend until smooth, using a spatula to scrape down the sides of your blender if necessary. Add a little milk or cream to thin as desired.

Store in a covered container in the fridge. Keeps for three days or more.

This cheese is great on baked potatoes, as a salad dressing (thinned as desired), on crackers, etc.

Try adding different herbs each time you make CC for a real chameleon recipe!

Alice's Wonderland Mushies

Combine in a quart jar with a tight-fitting lid

      4–6 T   OLIVE (or other) OIL
      1/4 c   HERB or WINE VINEGAR
      1/4 t each   SALT
                    TARRAGON
      1/8 t   GARLIC POWDER

Fill the jar with SLICED MUSHROOMS and SLICED RED ONIONS. Cover tightly and tilt around until all the veggies are well-coated.

Marinate for several hours at room temperature, tilting or turning the jar when you can.

Refrigerate until needed. Keeps a long time.

Serve as a salad on a bed of crisp greens, mix with cottage cheese, or use in ALICE'S COLOSSAL CHESHIRE CAT CREATION.

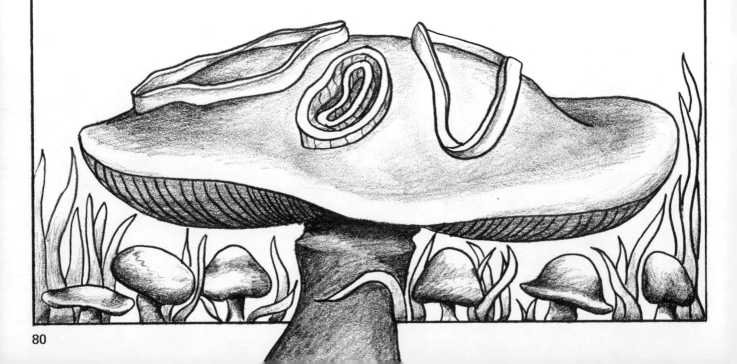

Alice's Colossal Cheshire Cat Creation

Create a masterpiece on a large platter using

TORN, CRISP SPINACH LEAVES

TOMATO QUARTERS

CUCUMBER AND ZUCCHINI ROUNDS

HARD-BOILED EGG HALVES or SLICES

OLIVES

Crumble FETA CHEESE (1-3 oz. per person) over the veggies.

Spoon on ALICE'S WONDERLAND MUSHIES, drizzling marinade over everything.

Add a heavy dark bread and some wine; then invite your friends in for a feast.

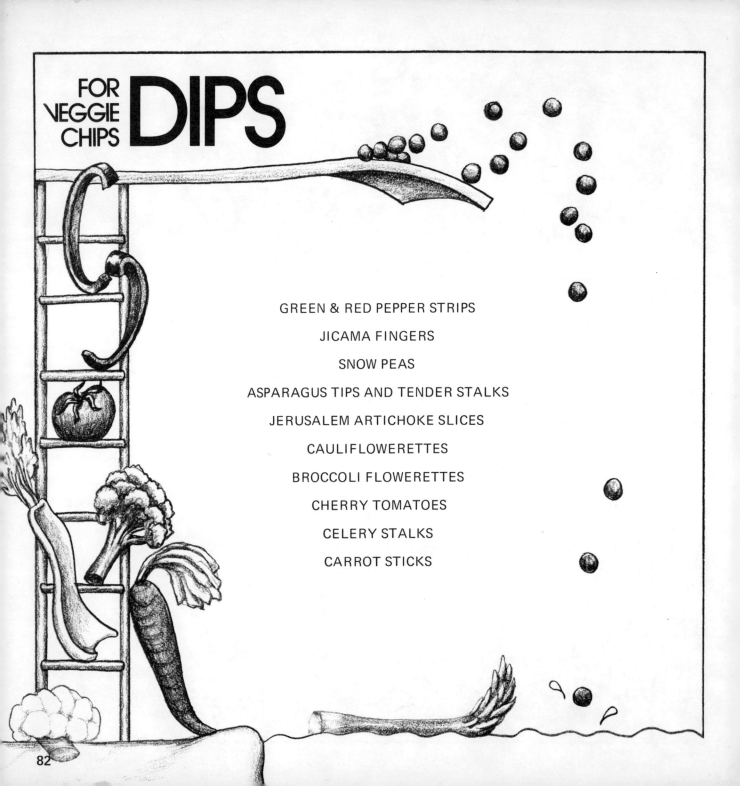

FOR VEGGIE CHIPS DIPS

GREEN & RED PEPPER STRIPS

JICAMA FINGERS

SNOW PEAS

ASPARAGUS TIPS AND TENDER STALKS

JERUSALEM ARTICHOKE SLICES

CAULIFLOWERETTES

BROCCOLI FLOWERETTES

CHERRY TOMATOES

CELERY STALKS

CARROT STICKS

OUR FAVORITE VEGGIE DIP

Mix together in a container
- 2/3 c MAYONNAISE
- 2/3 c YOGURT
- 1 T DRIED PARSLEY FLAKES
- 1 t DILL SEED or WEED
- 1/8–1/4 t each GARLIC POWDER
  - ONION POWDER
  - CELERY SEED
- SALT (to taste)

Don't dig in yet!! The flavors need to blend for several hours — especially if you use dill seed. Put on your will power and put that container in the fridge.

CHICK DIP

Combine in your blender
- 1 can (15 oz.) GARBANZO BEANS (also called CHICKPEAS), UNDRAINED*
- 3 T LEMON JUICE
- 1/4 c SESAME TAHINI
- 1/4 t CUMIN
- 1 clove GARLIC

Blend until silky smooth. Refrigerate several hours to let the flavors blend.

Serve garnished with parsley, whole garbanzo beans, sesame seeds, grated hard-boiled egg, chopped cucumber, or avocado bits.

*Adjust the consistency of CHICK DIP to your liking by varying the amount of bean liquor added.

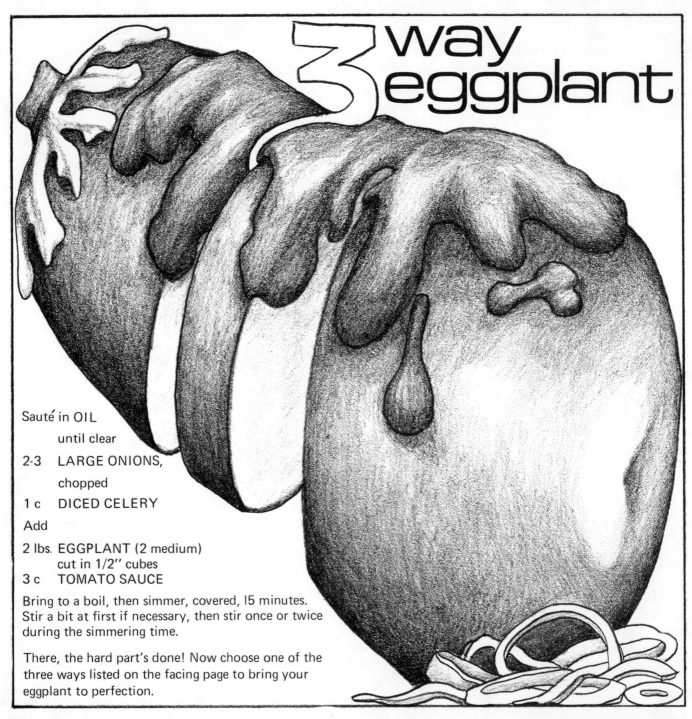

3 way eggplant

Sauté in OIL
    until clear

2-3 LARGE ONIONS,
    chopped

1 c DICED CELERY

Add

2 lbs. EGGPLANT (2 medium)
    cut in 1/2" cubes

3 c TOMATO SAUCE

Bring to a boil, then simmer, covered, 15 minutes.
Stir a bit at first if necessary, then stir once or twice
during the simmering time.

There, the hard part's done! Now choose one of the
three ways listed on the facing page to bring your
eggplant to perfection.

as a main dish veggie

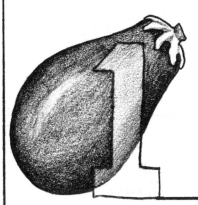

Continue simmering (covered) for another 20-30 minutes — until the eggplant is very tender.

SALT to taste.

Serve hot with cheeses and whole grain bread.

as a tangy appetizer

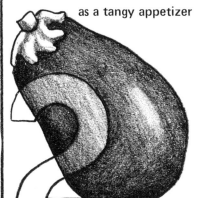

Add
1/4 c	RED WINE VINEGAR
2 T	CAPERS
1/2 t	SALT
2/3 c	CHOPPED BLACK OLIVES (one 4-1/2 oz. can)

Simmer (covered) for another 20-30 minutes — until the eggplant is very tender.

Refrigerate overnight in a covered container.

Serve at room temperature piled on sturdy crackers, or as a spooning hors d'oeuvre with broiled mushrooms.

as a cold vegetable salad

Continue simmering (covered) for another 20-30 minutes — until the eggplant is very tender.

Salt to taste.

Refrigerate in a covered container.

Serve cold or at room temperature on a bed or crisp lettuce leaves — or marble into cottage cheese or ricotta first, then serve.

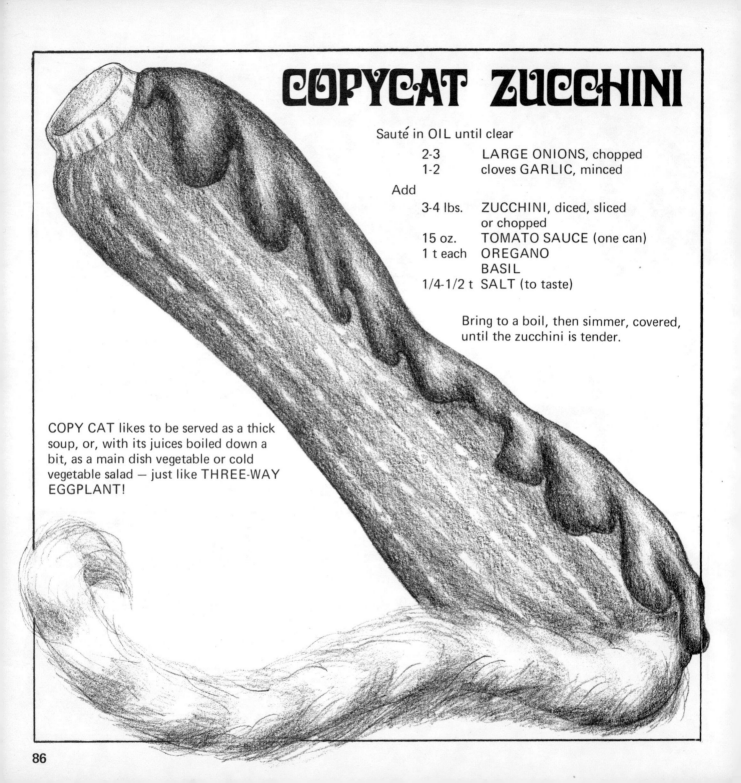

COPYCAT ZUCCHINI

Sauté in OIL until clear

2-3	LARGE ONIONS, chopped
1-2	cloves GARLIC, minced

Add

3-4 lbs.	ZUCCHINI, diced, sliced or chopped
15 oz.	TOMATO SAUCE (one can)
1 t each	OREGANO
	BASIL
1/4-1/2 t	SALT (to taste)

Bring to a boil, then simmer, covered, until the zucchini is tender.

COPY CAT likes to be served as a thick soup, or, with its juices boiled down a bit, as a main dish vegetable or cold vegetable salad — just like THREE-WAY EGGPLANT!

MERLIN'S MARINADE

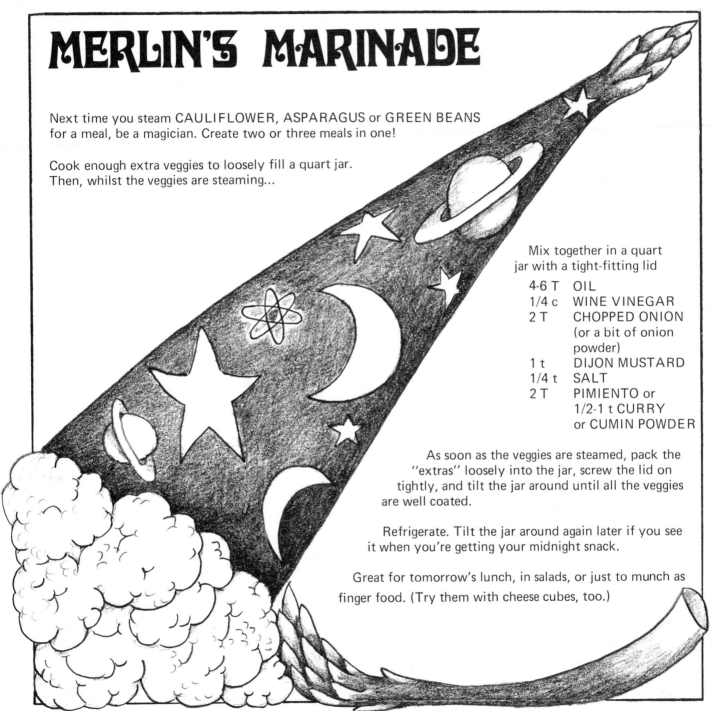

Next time you steam CAULIFLOWER, ASPARAGUS or GREEN BEANS for a meal, be a magician. Create two or three meals in one!

Cook enough extra veggies to loosely fill a quart jar.
Then, whilst the veggies are steaming...

Mix together in a quart jar with a tight-fitting lid

4-6 T	OIL
1/4 c	WINE VINEGAR
2 T	CHOPPED ONION (or a bit of onion powder)
1 t	DIJON MUSTARD
1/4 t	SALT
2 T	PIMIENTO or 1/2-1 t CURRY or CUMIN POWDER

As soon as the veggies are steamed, pack the "extras" loosely into the jar, screw the lid on tightly, and tilt the jar around until all the veggies are well coated.

Refrigerate. Tilt the jar around again later if you see it when you're getting your midnight snack.

Great for tomorrow's lunch, in salads, or just to munch as finger food. (Try them with cheese cubes, too.)

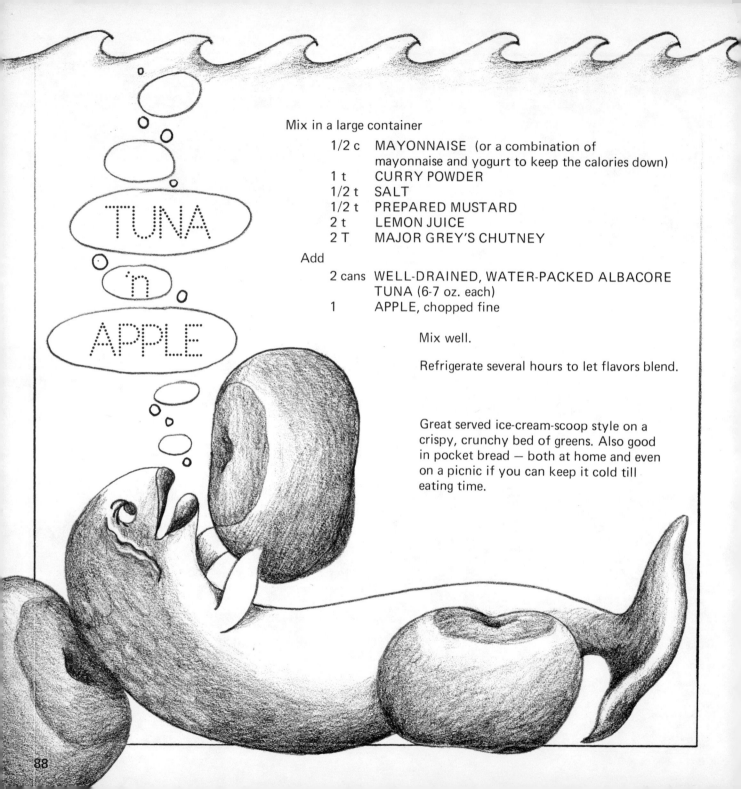

Mix in a large container

1/2 c	MAYONNAISE (or a combination of mayonnaise and yogurt to keep the calories down)
1 t	CURRY POWDER
1/2 t	SALT
1/2 t	PREPARED MUSTARD
2 t	LEMON JUICE
2 T	MAJOR GREY'S CHUTNEY

Add

2 cans	WELL-DRAINED, WATER-PACKED ALBACORE TUNA (6-7 oz. each)
1	APPLE, chopped fine

Mix well.

Refrigerate several hours to let flavors blend.

Great served ice-cream-scoop style on a crispy, crunchy bed of greens. Also good in pocket bread — both at home and even on a picnic if you can keep it cold till eating time.

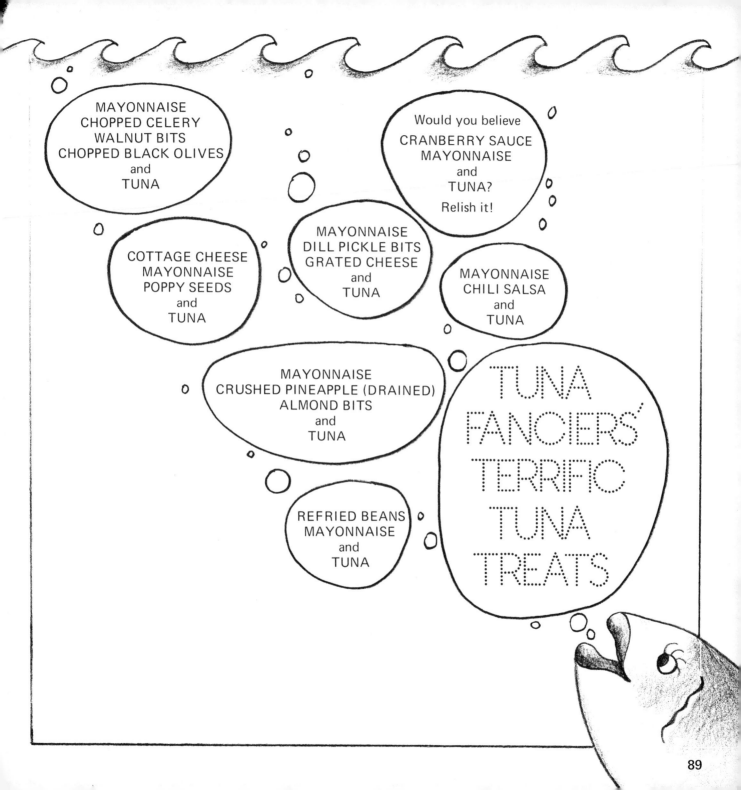

89

DO IT YOURSELF JELLO

SOFTEN 1T GELATIN in 1/2 c FRUIT JUICE

Homemade jello is easy and fun! Use the basic recipe above for the necessary proportions and then experiment to find your favorite varieties.

Add sweeteners, lemon juice, cinnamon, fruit pieces (except for fresh pineapple or fresh kiwi which both have an enzyme that'll keep your jello from doing its thing).

When you've got it just the way you want it, stir to blend completely.

Refrigerate, covered, to gel. (Stir at the syrupy stage if you added fruit and want it to be well distributed throughout the jello.)

Store in the fridge. Keeps well.

JELLO JUGGLES

Substitute frozen fruit juice for fresh. Use 3 parts water and 1 part concentrate — or for a fruitier taste use more concentrate and less water. For example, to make orange jello use 1/2 c frozen concentrate and 1-1/2 c water, or 3/4 c concentrate and 1-1/4 c water.

Substitute 1/2-1 c cottage cheese, ricotta, or yogurt for that much of the fruit juice or water in your recipe.

Let any jello mixture without fruit pieces thicken to a heavy syrup in the refrigerator. Then whip it with an electric mixer until it is fluffy. Refrigerate immediately for a WISPY WHIP or fold in some whipped cream and create a JELLO CREAM SUPREME.

DO IT DIVERSELY

HEAT TO DISOLVE..... add + 1½ c. FRUIT JUICE

MEGAN'S MELLOW JELLO
For Orange Juice Lovers

Soften 2 T GELATIN in 1 c WATER.

Heat to dissolve the gelatin completely.

Stir in (in order)
- 1 c   WATER
- 1 can   CRUSHED PINEAPPLE (with juice) (20 oz.)
- 1-1/2 c FROZEN ORANGE JUICE CONCENTRATE (two 6 oz. cans)

Refrigerate to set. Stir when syrupy to distribute pineapple or have a layered MELLOW. Delicious either way — especially with a dob of whipped cream and an oatmeal cookie!

GRAPINAPPLE GRATULATE
For Grapefruit Lovers

Soften 1 T GELATIN in 1/2 c WATER.

Heat to dissolve the gelatin completely.

Stir in (in order)
- 1 c   PINEAPPLE JUICE
- 3/4 c   WELL-DRAINED, CRUSHED PINEAPPLE
- 1/2 c   FROZEN GRAPEFRUIT JUICE CONCENTRATE (2/3 of a small 6 oz. can)

Refrigerate to set. Stir when syrupy to distribute pineapple — or have a layered GRAPINAPPLE GRATULATE.

If your tongue finds GRAPINAPPLE GRATULATE a little troublesome, introduce it to

TONGUE RECTIFYING RECIPE #1

Start out slowly saying
   grab an apple, grab an apple

Blend the above completely, saying more quickly with each beat
   grabanapple, grabanapple,
   grapanapple, grapinapple

Add, gradually
   gra
   chu
   let

Combine all and work until smooth. Store until needed. Keeps a long time.

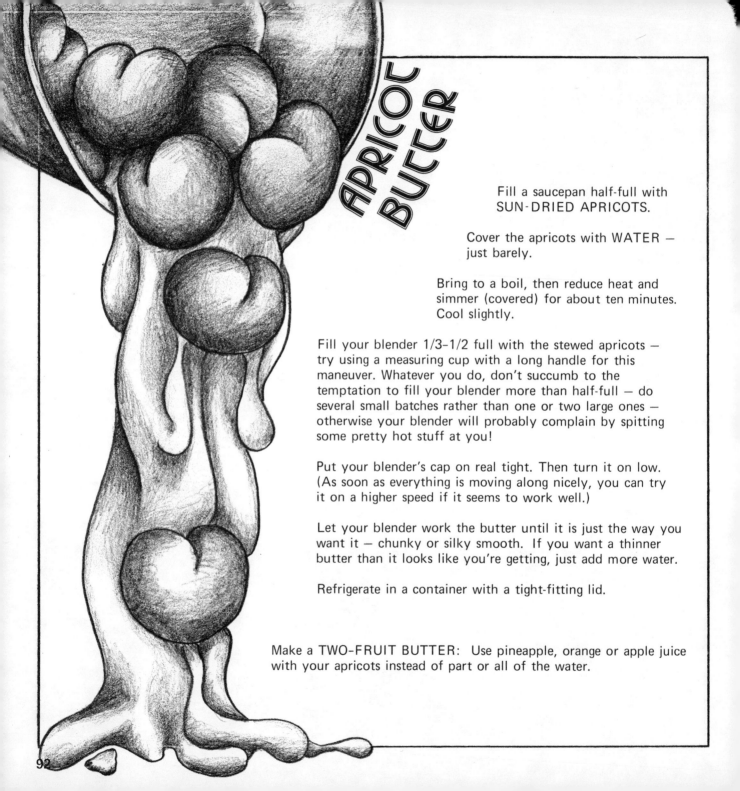

APRICOT BUTTER

Fill a saucepan half-full with
SUN-DRIED APRICOTS.

Cover the apricots with WATER —
just barely.

Bring to a boil, then reduce heat and
simmer (covered) for about ten minutes.
Cool slightly.

Fill your blender 1/3–1/2 full with the stewed apricots —
try using a measuring cup with a long handle for this
maneuver. Whatever you do, don't succumb to the
temptation to fill your blender more than half-full — do
several small batches rather than one or two large ones —
otherwise your blender will probably complain by spitting
some pretty hot stuff at you!

Put your blender's cap on real tight. Then turn it on low.
(As soon as everything is moving along nicely, you can try
it on a higher speed if it seems to work well.)

Let your blender work the butter until it is just the way you
want it — chunky or silky smooth. If you want a thinner
butter than it looks like you're getting, just add more water.

Refrigerate in a container with a tight-fitting lid.

Make a TWO-FRUIT BUTTER: Use pineapple, orange or apple juice
with your apricots instead of part or all of the water.

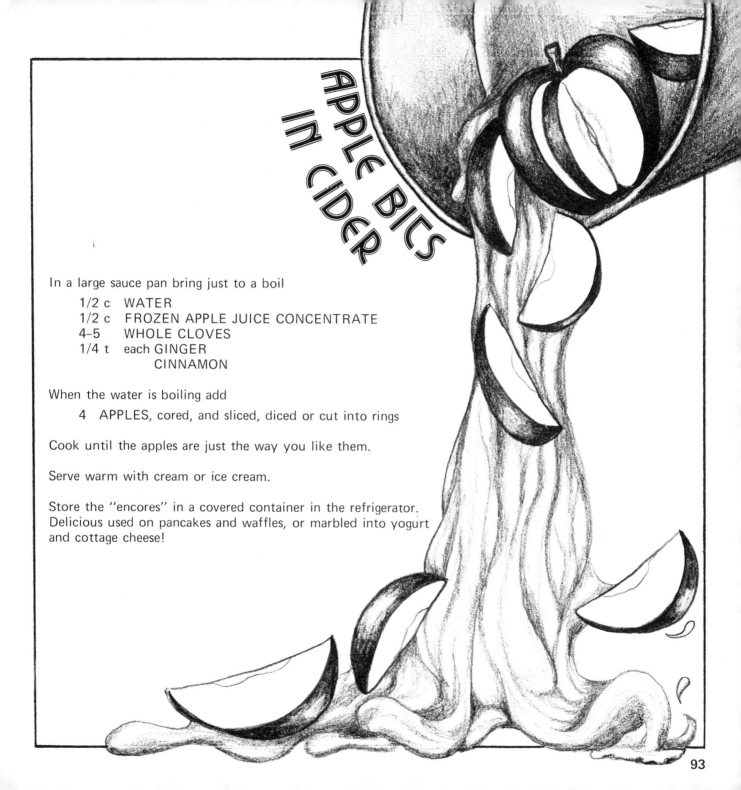

APPLE BITS IN CIDER

In a large sauce pan bring just to a boil

    1/2 c WATER
    1/2 c FROZEN APPLE JUICE CONCENTRATE
    4–5   WHOLE CLOVES
    1/4 t each GINGER
                 CINNAMON

When the water is boiling add

    4 APPLES, cored, and sliced, diced or cut into rings

Cook until the apples are just the way you like them.

Serve warm with cream or ice cream.

Store the "encores" in a covered container in the refrigerator.
Delicious used on pancakes and waffles, or marbled into yogurt
and cottage cheese!

93

SWEET TREATS AND GRATIFYING GOODIES

Captivatin' Carob Cwickies

Mix in a large bowl

      2/3 c   HONEY
      1 c   PEANUT BUTTER
      1/2 c CAROB POWDER

Add and mix again

      1/2 c   RAW SUNFLOWER SEEDS
      1/4–1/3 c   SESAME SEEDS
      1/3–1/2 c   UNSALTED SOY NUTS

Add enough INSTANT NONFAT POWDERED MILK
to firm up — about 2 c.

Knead until it holds together well.

Roll into balls or into one long log which can be cut
into bite-sized pieces after it chills in the fridge.

Store covered in the refrigerator.

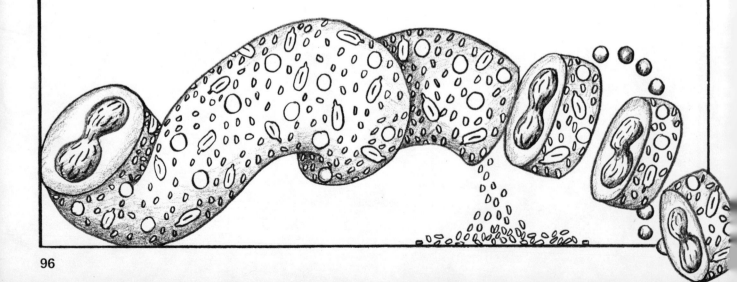

Great Balls O'Peanut Butter

Mix well in a large bowl

    1/4–1/2 c   HONEY
    1/2 c   PEANUT BUTTER

Add enough INSTANT NONFAT POWDERED MILK
to firm up — about 2 c.

Knead until it holds together well.

Roll into balls or into one long log which can be cut into
bite-sized pieces after it chills in the fridge.

Store covered in the fridge.

toothsomely tantalizing tahini tidbits

Mix well in a large bowl

      1/3 c   TAHINI or SESAME BUTTER
      3 T   HONEY
      1/2 t   CINNAMON

  Add and mix again

      1-1/2 c ROLLED OATS (in dry form)

Spoon out onto waxed paper and press firmly into a long log.
(You may need to sprinkle on 1–2 T WATER to help your
TTTT's stick together.)

Refrigerate until firm, then cut and mold into bite-sized pieces.

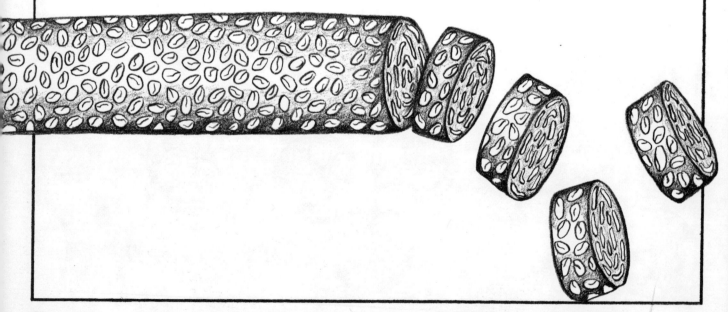

palate pleasin' peanut butter prunes

Mix well in a large bowl

     1 c   PEANUT BUTTER
     1/2 c STEWED PRUNES (about 10)
     1/4 c HONEY

  Add and mix again

     1/2 c ROLLED OATS (in dry form)

Add enough INSTANT NONFAT POWDERED MILK
to firm up — about 1/4 c.

Spoon out onto waxed paper and press into a long log.

Refrigerate until firm, then cut and mold into bite-sized
pieces.

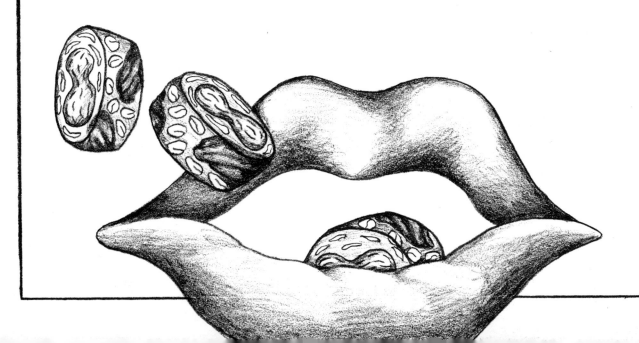

FARMHOUSE SUMMER CHEESE

Find a very clean jar with a tight-fitting lid **and** a covered pan that the jar will fit comfortably in when the pan has its hat on.

Pour into the jar

    2 c HALF AND HALF
    2 T BUTTERMILK (Be sure it's your favorite brand.)

Put the lid on the jar tightly and set it in the pan.

Fill the pan slowly with hot tap water until the water level is even with that of the Half and Half in the jar.

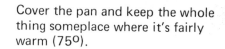

Cover the pan and keep the whole thing someplace where it's fairly warm (75°).

When the Half and Half becomes custard-like (in 12-15 hours), remove the jar from the pan and refrigerate.

Keeps about 10 days in the fridge. If the whey separates out a bit after the cheese sits for awhile, just stir it back in before serving.

Use as is on fruits and veggies (great with cranberry sauce), or try in HERBED or DESSERT SUMMER CHEESE.

DESSERT SUMMER CHEESE

Mix one cup of SUMMER CHEESE with
1/8 t	SALT
1 T	HONEY (or to taste)

For variation try adding
- allspice, cinnamon, nutmeg, etc.
- or a few drops of vanilla
- or 1 T finely chopped crystallized ginger
- or 1/4 t almond extract
  - 1/2 c toasted almond bits
- or frozen orange juice concentrate
    (to taste)

Ladle over chilled orange sections,
strawberries, and/or banana rounds.
Heavenly!

HERBED SUMMER CHEESE

Mix one cup of SUMMER CHEESE with
3/8 t	SALT (or to taste)	
1/4 t	each	BASIL
		TARRAGON
		THYME
dash	each	GARLIC POWDER
		ONION POWDER

Use on crisp greens as a salad dressing or
serve in a "dunking bowl" with raw
veggie chips.

GRANDMA'S WHOLE EGG CUSTARD

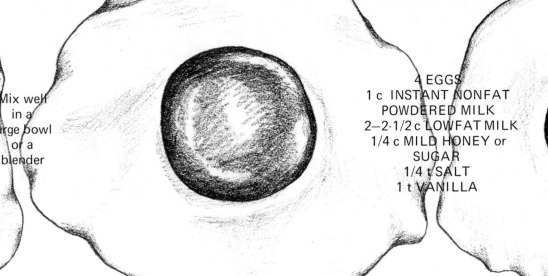

Mix well
in a
large bowl
or a
blender

4 EGGS
1 c INSTANT NONFAT
POWDERED MILK
2—2-1/2 c LOWFAT MILK
1/4 c MILD HONEY or
SUGAR
1/4 t SALT
1 t VANILLA

Pour the egg mixture into a shallow 1 quart baking dish that fits comfortably in a large baking pan with at least 2″ sides.

Set the baking dish into the pan and then put them in the oven.

Fill the large pan with water to within 1/2″ of its rim.

Bake at 300°F until a knife blade inserted in the center of the custard comes out clean (about one hour and fifteen minutes).

Remove the custard from its water bath and cool at room temperature on a wire rack.

Refrigerate as soon as the custard is cool.

GRANDDAUGHTER'S VARIATIONS

Substitute 1 c of applesauce for 1 c of the milk called for in Granny's recipe. If the applesauce is sweet enough, you'll be able to reduce the amount of sugar or honey she calls for, too.

Add 4 oz. dates (1/2 c chopped). Either whiz them in the blender with the rest of the ingredients until everything is quite smooth or just stir them in after everything is well blended. Try reducing the sweetening in this recipe too — especially if you whirl the dates smooth.

BANANA POPS!

Peel a few MEDIUM-RIPE BANANAS.

Cut each in half and insert an ice cream stick in the cut end.

Freeze firm on a plate or pan.

When frozen, dip each BANANA POP in CAROB SAUCE, MAPLE SYRUP or HONEY thinned with warm water. (Brush or spoon the sauce on if you're just doing a few.)

Roll in CHOPPED NUTS, GRANOLA, OATS or COOKIE CRUMBS.

Enjoy right away or put in an airtight container and return to the freezer.

Use within a couple months for best banana flavor.

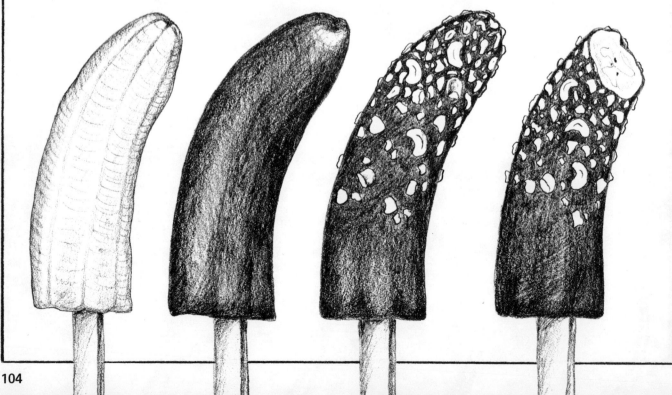

FROSTY FEAST

THOMPSON SEEDLESS GRAPES and BING CHERRIES are both delicious to munch when they're frosty. Just

Wash and drain the fruit well.

Arrange it on a cookie sheet in a single layer.
(Stem the grapes but leave the stems on the
cherries for extra fun.)

Freeze solid, uncovered.

Package the frozen fruit quickly in an
airtight container and return to the freezer.

Use within 2–3 months for best flavor.

Try these glacial gems with cheese and nuts for a company dessert. The cherries are especially pretty if you let them frost over a bit before you serve them. Don't let them defrost completely, though, or their delightfully chilly crunch will become a mealy mush.

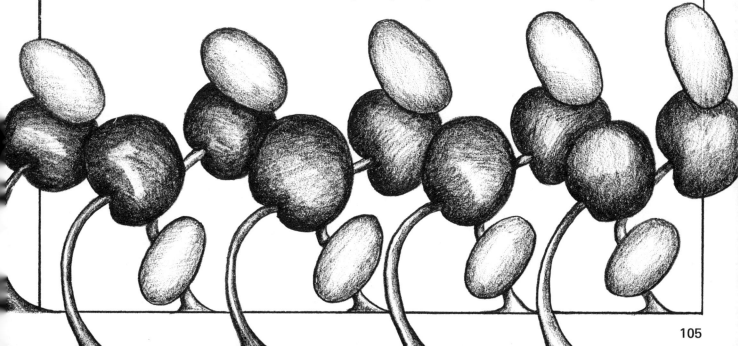

Mix in a container with a cover

    1 can (20 oz.)   CRUSHED PINEAPPLE
    a few tablespoons   FROZEN ORANGE JUICE CONCENTRATE
                        (optional)

Snap on the cover and freeze till the mixture is frosty cold.

Serve in stemmed goblets. Pass bowls of WHIPPED CREAM and
CHOPPED NUTS to garnish. Elegantly easy...

FROSTY THE PINEAPPLE

Mix well in your blender

      2 c   PLAIN YOGURT
      3 oz.   FROZEN ORANGE JUICE CONCENTRATE
             (1/2 a small can)
      1/2 t VANILLA

Pour into popsicle molds and freeze solid.

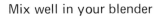

YUMMY YOGSICLE

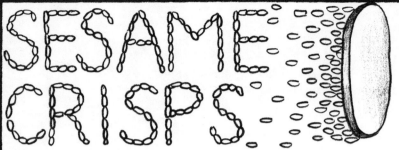

SESAME CRISPS

Mix well in a large bowl

1/2 c	OIL
2	EGGS
1 t	VANILLA
1 c	DARK BROWN SUGAR *
1/2 t	SALT
1 t	CINNAMON
1/4 t	NUTMEG

Add and mix to blend

1 c	WHOLE WHEAT FLOUR
3/4 t	SODA
1 c	SESAME SEEDS
1 c	ROLLED OATS (in dry form)

Drop by teaspoonfuls onto a cookie sheet.
Bake at 350°F for 10-18 minutes.
Makes about 40 cookies.

* or 3/4 c honey.

For busy people who've sometimes got the time, and often got the inclination...

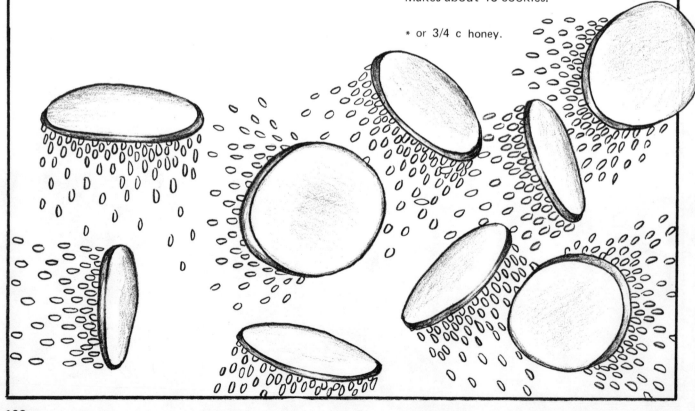

ELLIOTO'S OAT CHIPPERS

For busy people who've sometimes got the time, and often got the inclination...

Mix well in a large bowl

1/2 c	OIL
2	EGGS
3/4 t	SALT
3/4–1 c	DARK BROWN SUGAR *
1 t	VANILLA

Add and mix again

1 c	WHOLE WHEAT FLOUR
3/4 t	SODA

Finally add and mix (one cup at a time)

3 c	ROLLED OATS (in dry form)
1/2 c	CAROB or CHOCOLATE CHIPS

Drop by teaspoonfuls onto a cookie sheet. Flatten a bit if desired.

Bake at 350° for 10-18 minutes.

Makes about 50 cookies.

* or 3/4 c honey.

CHEESY POPCORN

Pop a popper full of POPCORN.

Spread it out in a large shallow baking pan. (Send any tough or tired ol' kernels that try to pull rank on you back to the barracks!)

Sprinkle generously with one of your favorite GRATED CHEESES.

Warm in a 350° oven just until the cheese is melted.

Cool a bit and dig in!

Serve CHEESY POPCORN with WITCH'S APPLE BREW

Combine in a saucepan

4 c	APPLE JUICE or CIDER (or 1 c FROZEN APPLE JUICE CONCENTRATE and 3 c WATER)
6	WHOLE CLOVES
2''	CINNAMON STICK

Bring almost to a boil, then cover and simmer till the spice is right — about ten minutes.

Try simmering with a few raisins and/or a slice or two of lemon sometime, too.

For each serving mix in a bowl

2 T	PLAIN YOGURT
some	HONEY and/or LEMON JUICE (optional)
2 T	ROLLED OATS (in dry form)
some	CHOPPED, TOASTED ALMONDS
1	APPLE, chopped, grated, or "moulied"*

Don't let Dean have all the fun! Create your own muesli — how about adding some

raisins or currants
granola
mixed nuts and seeds
carob powder

DEAN'S MAGNIFICENT MUESLI

*See footnote page 74.

APPENDIX

THE FOUR FOOD GROUPS MAGIC NUMBER SYSTEM

THE MAGIC NUMBERS:

          4-4-2-2 for adults
          4-4-3-2 for kids and pregnant women
          4-4-4-2 for teens and nursing mothers

WHAT THE NUMBERS MEAN:

          4-Four servings from the Whole Grain Bread and Cereal Group
          4-Four servings from the Fruit and Vegetable Group
          2-Two (or three or four) servings from the Milk Group
          2-Two servings from the Protein Group

HOW TO USE THE NUMBERS:

          First choose the magic numbers appropriate for you. Then choose a typical food day and ask yourself the following four questions about the foods you ate during that day:

          1. Did I have four servings from the Whole Grain Bread and Cereal Group today?
          2. Did I have at least four servings from the Fruit and Vegetable Group today?
          3. Did I have 2 (3 or 4, as appropriate) servings of Milk Group foods today?
          4. Did I have 2 servings of Protein Group foods today?

HOW TO RECOGNIZE A SERVING SIZE:

Some examples of one serving from the Bread and Cereal Group:

1 slice of bread   1/2–3/4 c cooked cereal, rice or pasta
1 tortilla
5 crackers (2" x 2")

Some examples of one serving from the Fruit and Vegetable Group:

1/2 c cooked fruit or veggie
1 c raw fruit or veggie
1 medium out-of-hand fruit or veggie
1/2 grapefruit
Be sure that at least one of your selections is a good source of Vitamin C—like broccoli, citrus fruit, bell pepper—and that one is either deep green or yellow-orange in color for vitamin A.

Some examples of one serving from the Milk Group:

1 c (8 oz.) milk, buttermilk, yogurt
1 oz. (generous) hard cheese (like cheddar)
1 c custard or milk pudding
1-1/3 c cottage cheese
1/3 c dry instant powdered milk
If you are an inveterate milk avoider, try tofu, lots of greens (like collards, kale, mustard, turnip), broccoli, Chinese cabbage, corn tortillas, or soy beans to increase your calcium intake.

Some examples of one serving from the Protein Group:

2 eggs
1 c cooked dried peas or beans
4 T peanut butter
1/3 c nuts
8 oz. tofu
2-3 oz. fish

A day in the Commercial Fast-Food Syndrome would probably find you overloaded in the Protein Group and short in both the Fruit/Vegetable Group and the Milk Group. When this happens excess protein foods are needlessly used for energy—or worse yet, stored as fat. Also, the requirements for the several important nutrients found in the Fruit/Vegetable Group and the Milk Group are not met. The Foodbook not only helps you meet your Protein and Bread/Cereal Group needs, but also offers many fruit-, vegetable- and milk-based recipes to help you balance your day tastily and easily.

INDEX

THE BUSY PEOPLE'S NATURALLY NUTRITIOUS, DECIDEDLY DELICIOUS, FAST FOODBOOK
makes an inimitable gift. Share your find with a friend!

Just fill out the form and send it along with $4.95 (plus $.50 for handling)
per copy to

fresh
press
774 Allen Court
Palo Alto
California
94303

- - - - cut here - cut here - - - -

Please send me_____copies of THE BUSY PEOPLE'S NATURALLY NUTRITIOUS, DECIDEDLY
DELICIOUS, FAST FOODBOOK. I have enclosed $_____.

NAME _____

ADDRESS _____

CITY _____STATE_____ZIP_____

cut here

Please send me_____copies of THE BUSY PEOPLE'S NATURALLY NUTRITIOUS, DECIDEDLY DELICIOUS, FAST FOODBOOK. I have enclosed $_____.

NAME _____

ADDRESS _____

CITY _____STATE _____ ZIP _____

THE BUSY PEOPLE'S NATURALLY NUTRITIOUS, DECIDEDLY DELICIOUS, FAST FOODBOOK makes an inimitable gift. Share your find with a friend!

Just fill out the form and send it along with $4.95 (plus $.50 for handling) per copy to

fresh press

774 Allen Court
Palo Alto
California
94303